SO TO SPEAK

Orsa Maggiore

Pol.

Cassiopea

Shoot for the stars

SO TO SPEAK

11,000 EXPRESSIONS
THAT'LL KNOCK YOUR SOCKS OFF

Shirley Kobliner and Harold Kobliner, PhD

Tiller Press

New York   London   Toronto   Sydney   New Delhi

TILLER PRESS

An Imprint of Simon & Schuster, Inc.
1230 Avenue of the Americas
New York, NY 10020

First Tiller Press trade paperback edition December 2020

TILLER PRESS and colophon are trademarks of Simon & Schuster, Inc.

For information about special discounts for bulk purchases, please contact Simon & Schuster Special Sales at 1-866-506-1949 or business@simonandschuster.com.

The Simon & Schuster Speakers Bureau can bring authors to your live event. For more information or to book an event, contact the Simon & Schuster Speakers Bureau at 1-866-248-3049 or visit our website at www.simonspeakers.com.

Design by Pentagram

Manufactured in the United States of America

10 9 8 7 6 5 4 3 2 1

Library of Congress Cataloging-in-Publication Data

Names: Kobliner, Shirley, author. | Kobliner, Harold, author.
Title: So to speak : 11,000 expressions that'll knock your socks off / by Shirley Kobliner and Harold Kobliner, Ph.D.
Other titles: 11,000 expressions that'll knock your socks off
Description: New York, NY : Tiller Press, November 2020.
Identifiers: LCCN 2020023123 (print) | LCCN 2020023124 (ebook) |
ISBN 9781982163761 (paperback) | ISBN 9781982163778 (ebook)
Subjects: LCSH: English language—Idioms.
Classification: LCC PE1460 .K73 2020 (print) | LCC PE1460 (ebook) | DDC 423/.13—dc23
LC record available at https://lccn.loc.gov/2020023123
LC ebook record available at https://lccn.loc.gov/2020023124

ISBN 978-1-9821-6376-1
ISBN 978-1-9821-6377-8 (ebook)

DEDICATION

We dedicate this book to our darling grandchildren, Rebecca,
Adam, Benjamin, Joshua, Sarah, and Jacob, who are more fun than
a barrel of monkeys—but also know that sometimes it's necessary to
do what you have to do, not what you want to do. From generation to
generation, we hope this book continues to spark your love of language,
your appreciation for the art of conversation, and your zest for lifelong
learning. We also know it'll remind you of all the fun times we had
coming up with these expressions together.

Love,
Grandma Shirley and Grandpa Harold

And to our children and children-in-law who have made us proud:
We think you're all the cat's meow.

Love,
Mom and Dad/Shirley and Harold

CONTENTS

THE EXPRESSIONS

Balance the books

THE STORY BEHIND
SO TO SPEAK

"It looks like you all have ants in your pants!" said my wife, Shirley. We were reading to our grandson's kindergarten class, when we noticed the children starting to squirm.

"Ants in your pants?" asked a tiny boy.

"That's funny!" yelled a girl with a big grin.

Shirley closed the book, smiled, and explained the unfamiliar expression. "It means you're fidgeting, as if there were ants crawling up the leg of your pants."

"Ewwwwww," said a boy. At that moment, everyone—including the teacher—started to laugh.

Sensing she was on a roll, Shirley asked, "Can anyone think of another expression about bugs or insects?"

"There's busy as a bee!" I chimed in. Several children nodded.

"My mom says I'm a social butterfly!" said a girl.

"Snug as a bug in a rug," exclaimed our grandson, Jacob. "Grandpa taught me that!"

Soon, several children were flapping their wings and buzzing around the story-time rug as they shouted out expressions. For two educators—Shirley had been a teacher, and I a middle school principal—it was a memorable moment.

As we drove home, we couldn't stop giggling. After I pulled into the driveway, Shirley turned to me with bright eyes. "You know," she said, "this would make a great book."

I had been thinking the exact same thing.

Thirteen years, twenty-six legal pads, and countless conversations later, we ended up with the book you now hold in your hands. It is the largest collection of its kind, with more than eleven thousand English-language expressions curated and categorized in a uniquely entertaining way.

From the start, we made a conscious decision not to use the internet to find new expressions, and not to look at other collections. Every expression we include here is one we heard with our own ears or saw with our own eyes—on radio and TV, at the theater, at lectures and debates, in everyday interactions, in books and newspapers we were reading. We took suggestions from family, friends, and people we met in our daily lives, jotting down each new expression on the crisp white shirt cardboards from our dry cleaner that Shirley repurposed as scrap paper. (We soon moved on to those many legal pads, and eventually a computer spreadsheet, to keep track.) We also drew upon our own memories.

During the decade-plus of gathering, culling, and categorizing, we hit some milestones.

Send up a trial balloon

At five thousand expressions, our son-in-law helped us weed out duplicates by coming up with an algorithm so that each expression appears only once in the book. And as we neared the nine-thousand-expression mark, we offered our grandkids a modest bounty (a dollar per new expression). All in all, this project has been a labor of love (to use a favorite expression), and a true celebration of the love of language with the love of my life.

After sixty-five wonderful years of marriage, I lost Shirley in 2016. There is not a day that goes by that I don't miss her immensely. At first, I felt I couldn't continue the project without her. But during a gathering at our home after she passed away, friends began spontaneously sharing expressions in her honor, and I knew that I needed to finish our book.

Every time I hear an expression, I feel Shirley's humor, beauty, and intelligence. This book comes from both of us, with warm wishes. Our hope is that it keeps you on your toes, jogs fun memories, and knocks your socks off!

Harold Kobliner

The third wheel

WHAT MAKES *SO TO SPEAK* FUN

We use expressions all the time, often without much thought. When you feel sick, you're **under the weather**; when you feel great, you're **on top of the world**! If you don't speak up, it could be that **the cat's got your tongue**, or maybe it's just **a frog in your throat**. You may be fine with **half a loaf**, or you may insist on **the whole enchilada**. No matter if you're **a smart cookie** or a tough one, you—and most everyone you know—has a veritable smorgasbord of expressions stored deep in your brain.

But expressions are more than just words; they tell a story of who you are, where you lived, and when you grew up. Someone who says a friend is **all hat and no cattle** is likely **from a different neck of the woods** than the person who asks **What am I, chopped liver?** Expressions also offer a clue as to when you **came of age:** if you ask for **the skinny** on a rumor you hear, you're almost certainly **longer in the tooth** than if you ask someone to **spill the tea**.

Okay, now you're thinking, that all makes sense. But what do you do with a book of thousands of expressions?

Here's where we show you the ropes.

First, try flipping through the book breezily, moving among its sixty-seven carefully curated, sometimes-quirky categories of expressions, from "Animals" to "Arts & Entertainment"; from "Colors" to "Gambling"; from "Love & Kisses" to "Royalty" to "Science & Technology." You may start to notice that each expression is categorized based on a key word rather than its overall meaning, leading to some entertaining results. Take the expression "**a sting operation.**" You might think it goes in the "Law" category, since it conjures up an image of FBI agents going undercover to infiltrate a criminal enterprise, but that's not the case. Because the expression pivots on the word "sting," we placed it in the "Birds, Bats & Insects" category—which includes close to two hundred other expressions, some obvious (**busy as a bee, a wild-goose chase, fly the coop**) and others less so (**a chick flick, a flea market, search the web**). For us, debating with each other over where to place each expression was incredibly time-consuming—but also one of the most fulfilling aspects of creating *So to Speak*. (That said, since categorizing expression is more of an art than a science, we won't be surprised if you take issue with some of our choices!)

Meanwhile, if you're itching to tap into your inner linguist, go to the back of the book to find blank pages for recording your favorite expressions, jotting down ones we missed, or even creating expressions of your own. You might find some surprises along the way. Take the case of our friend Diane, who loved using her mother's old Irish saying "**as fast as O'Grady's dog**" to describe someone who moves quickly, as in: "Right when the waiter brought the check, Michelle left the restaurant **as fast as O'Grady's dog.**" One day, Diane met her mother's childhood friend, who launched into a story about the infamous neighborhood dog that always ran away from its owners, the O'Gradys. It suddenly hit Diane that **as fast as O'Grady's dog** wasn't an old Irish expression at all—it was a personal one known only to her mother's family and neighbors!

Once you've dipped your toes in, you'll see that *So to Speak* is a catalyst for endless conversations among people of all ages—and some of the most fun can be had by reading it aloud with friends and family. Sharing expressions is a low-pressure way for children and parents to connect, and to unplug from everyday life. (Studies show that this type of interaction tends to reduce family stress and improve kids' behavior overall.) Whether it's

grandparents offering up their favorite expressions from childhood, kids helping adults keep up with the latest lingo, lifelong friends reminiscing about old times, or new friends swapping sayings from their varied backgrounds, *So to Speak* will spur discussion and debate, while encouraging the art of listening and celebrating the joy of words.

A lounge lizard

PLAYING GAMES WITH *SO TO SPEAK*

Here are twenty-five games you can play with *So to Speak* to turn gatherings of friends or family into raucous game nights. Take a look:

1. FAST TALKER.

Choose a category and set a timer for one minute. When the timer starts, each player yells out expressions that fit into that category—and whoever yells the most in that one minute wins. (So, if you picked the "Body" category—which has more than eight hundred expressions—you'd think of ones like **tongue-tied**, **head honcho**, **break a leg**, **go to the head of the class**, and **left bone dry**.) To bump it up a level, choose a single word that's popular within a given category—for example, the word *eye* from the "Body" category—and see who can come up with the most expressions (like: **an eye for an eye**, **eyes on the prize**, **in the blink of an eye**, **the apple of my eye**, **an eagle eye**, **eyes in the back of your head**). You can make this even harder by choosing a more obscure category like "Containers," which includes a **basket case**, **a melting pot**, **a mixed bag**, **case closed**, **the bucket list**, **keep a lid on it**, and **hit the sack**.

2. CLUE ME IN.

Put players into two teams and agree on a category in *So to Speak*—making sure all players know what it is. One player from each team will go head-to-head. Have these players turn to a page in the chosen category. Set a timer for two minutes and—starting from the top left of the page and working down the

list of expressions in order—have Player A describe each expression to their team, but without using any of the words in the expression itself. (The player might describe **brave as a lion** by saying it's "when you have the courage of a big cat.") After the two minutes are over, count how many expressions Team A got, then set the timer for two minutes and let Player B continue by describing the list for their team. Go back and forth until the entire category list is done, at which point the team with the higher tally wins!

3. REAL OR FAKE.

A good poker face helps here. Have a player flip through *So to Speak* and either find an expression or just pretend to do so and make one up. The player announces the expression (whether legit or invented) to the group, and each of the other players vote on whether it's real or fake. (For instance, is the saying **reliable as Epsom salt** a real one? And what about **a yellow dog contract**?) After the player reveals whether their expression is real or not, tally up the number of incorrect guesses and move on to the next player. After each player has had two turns, the player who received the most incorrect guesses wins. (In case you're wondering, **reliable as Epsom salt** is fake, and **a yellow dog contract** is real.)

4. TIME TO ACT OUT.

For this expressions-oriented take on charades, start by breaking up into two teams. Choose one player from each team to be performers and have those

A fishy story

players decide on a category, which they then reveal to the group as a clue. Next, the performers silently agree on an expression and go head-to-head acting it out—without making any sounds! The first team to guess the expression wins.

5. LIST-OFF.

This is like FAST TALKER but working in teams and using paper and pencil. Put players into two teams, open up *So to Speak*, and agree on a category. Set a timer for two minutes and see which team can think of the most expressions in the chosen category. But be careful—if your team writes down an expression that doesn't exist, subtract one from your total count.

6. TOMATO, TO-MAH-TO, POTATO, PO-TAH-TO.

There are no winners or losers in this game—but it's a great way to learn how language changes over time. Break players into two teams, making sure that each team has members of different generations (if possible). Teams must think of one old-school and one modern-day expression that mean the same thing. (For instance, Grandpa might call Grandma **sweetie pie**, while you call your significant other **BAE**—or maybe your great aunt's **knee-slapper** makes you **LOL**.) Once each team thinks of its pair of expressions, present them aloud to the group.

7. SONGBOOK.

This one works best by splitting the group into two teams. Have each team peruse *So to Speak* and choose three expressions from any category in the book.

(Let's say you choose **get under my skin**, **have egg on your face**, and **an olive branch**.) Set a timer for ten minutes, and let each team write a song—we're thinking a parody of a well-known song, but you can also make up one of your own—making sure to incorporate all the chosen expressions. (Maybe you'll sing, "Welcome to the Hotel California, such a lovely place, with egg on my face . . .") Each team presents its song to the group, and everyone votes on the winner.

8. ALL'S FAIR IN LOVE AND EXPRESSIONS.

This one, a take on *The Newlywed Game*, is great if you're in a group of couples. To start, have one member of each couple leave the room—and make sure they can't hear what's going on. With the remaining players, come up with a personal relationship question; for example, "What is your partner like in the morning?" Look through *So to Speak* to find three expressions that answer the question; you might choose **bright-eyed and bushy-tailed**, **in a snit**, and **dog tired**. Ask players to choose one expression that best describes their partner, then invite the partners back into the room. Share the question and the three possible answers. Go couple by couple to see if the partners can guess how they were described by their significant others—giving a point to each couple that guesses correctly. Keep playing, rotating who has to leave the room, until one couple scores five points.

9. YOU CAN READ ME LIKE A BOOK.

Have one player secretly pick another player in the group—let's say Mom picks Grandpa—and hand her *So to Speak*. Let Mom peruse the book to find three expressions that describe Grandpa, which can be either complimentary or not so much. (Maybe she chooses to describe him as **wise as an owl**, **a family man**, and **slow on the uptake**.) Have Mom share her chosen expressions with the group, and then give every other player a chance to guess the person she's describing. Once everyone guesses, Mom reveals the truth—and anyone who guessed Grandpa gets a point. (As a bonus: If Grandpa guessed himself correctly, he gets an extra point! To thine own self be true, after all.) Play until one player scores ten points.

10. SPEAKING IN TONGUES.

This game tests who can keep a conversation going the longest while only using expressions. Pick a random page in *So to Speak* and have two players sit side-by-side, so that each player can see the page. Set a timer for one minute, and let each player silently review the page to get familiar with its expressions. When the timer is up, the players enter into a conversation with each other—and are required to insert an expression from the page into each sentence they speak, without repeating any expression already said. (Players can keep consulting the page for help.) Player A might say, "Stop being such **a wet noodle**!" And Player B might respond with, "Why are you all **up in my grill**?"—you get the idea. A player wins when their opponent fails to work an expression into a sentence of the conversation within ten seconds.

11. QUIPPED FROM THE HEADLINES.

Who says expressions can't be topical? For this game, one player acts as emcee and presents a recent newspaper story to the group. (For instance, say the emcee shares news that Prince Harry and Meghan Markle just started their own reality show.) Next, pass *So to Speak* around the group of other players, giving each player thirty seconds to silently choose an expression to describe the news story.

Once everyone's had a chance to choose, each player presents his expression to the emcee, who then picks their favorite, declaring the winner of the round. (One player might say that Harry and Meghan will be **rolling in the dough**, and another that their show will cause them **a royal pain**.)

12. ALPHABET SOUP.

This game starts with a question to the group, such as: "What are ways to describe a fun night out?" Put players into two teams, give each team a pencil and a pad of paper, and have each write the letters of the alphabet from A to Z vertically on the left side of a sheet of paper. Then it's a race to see which team is quickest to fill in one expression (answering the original question) starting with each letter of the alphabet. (Maybe a fun night out is **awesome sauce**, a **barrel of laughs**, and has you **caught up in the moment**—you get it!) While thinking up expressions, each team gets *So to Speak* for sixty seconds at a time, passing it back and forth for help. First team to complete the alphabet wins.

13. PASSWORD FOR WORDS.

Those who remember the classic game show *Password* will love this one—it's the same thing, but with expressions. Break players into two teams, with each team choosing a player to go head-to-head against another, and have these players silently agree on one expression from *So to Speak* (like **cool as a cucumber**). Then let Player A say just one word to try to get their team to guess the expression (maybe they say "nonchalant," but their team can't guess the expression). Next, Player B says just one more word to try to get their team to guess the expression (maybe they say "pickle," and their team is able to guess the expression—score one for Team B!). Keep playing until one team gets to ten points.

14. WHAT'S YOUR STORY?

This game gives everyone a shot at being an author. Give each player a pencil and a pad. Pass *So to Speak* around the circle, letting each player pick a random page, choose an expression from the page, and read that expression aloud while all the other players, including the reader, write it down. (Each player needs to choose an expression they know, and then explain its meaning to the group.) All players will end up with the same list of expressions on their sheet of paper. Set a timer for ten minutes and have each player write a short story that uses all the expressions—and maybe even uses a few extras for added effect. When the timer goes off, take turns having all the players read their stories aloud—and then let everyone vote on their favorite. The player with the most votes wins the round, and the game ends once one player wins three rounds.

15. QUICK ON THE DRAW.

This one's perfect for budding artists. You'll need two pads of paper, pencils, and a wild imagination. Break players into two teams. Choose two players as artists— one from each team—to go head-to-head. One artist picks a random page of *So to Speak*, and the other artist closes their eyes and points to an expression— then both look at the expression without saying it out loud. The artists then draw the expression for their teams, without any talking or writing out words. The team that correctly guesses the expression first wins the round, and the team that wins five rounds first— choosing new artists every round—wins the game. (Some expressions will be easy to draw—think **a snake in the grass**—and others less so. For instance, how would you draw **a disappearing act**?)

16. RHYMIN' SIMON.

Gather all players in a circle, open *So to Speak*, and agree on an expression as a group. (Let's take **on the chopping block**.) Give everyone two minutes on their own to think up other expressions that rhyme with the chosen phrase, using *So to Speak* as a resource. Have one player start things off by reading the original expression, then go around the circle with each player saying a new rhyming expression (how about **eat the clock** or **state of shock**). Each player's turn lasts ten seconds; if the player can't shout out a rhyme within that ten seconds, they're eliminated. The round continues until just

one player is left. Pick a new kick-off expression (preferably with a different rhyme scheme) for each round.

17. EGG HUNT.

This is perfect for the little ones in your family. You'll need a dozen or more plastic Easter eggs (the kind that open up), and just as many scraps of paper. Open *So to Speak* to the "House & Home" category, which is full of expressions about items around the house, and find expressions that correspond to various things in your home. Write these down on the scraps of paper, then put one scrap in each egg and hide the eggs near the corresponding household objects. (Maybe put **the greatest thing since sliced bread** by your toaster or hide **the breakfast of champions** in the cereal cabinet.) Then send your kids on an egg hunt, making sure to read and explain the expression inside each egg they discover. As a bonus, add candy!

18. FUNNY BUSINESS.

Calling all aspiring comedians—it's time to play expressions improv. Choose one person to play the director and have them turn to a random page in *So to Speak*. They then call out up to five expressions from the book, and the other players have to immediately jump into a comedy sketch incorporating the expressions they've just heard. To spice things up, the director—at any time—can throw out another batch of expressions, and the comedians need to adjust on the spot. This one's guaranteed to be **a laugh a minute**.

19. MEMORY GRID.

This one is good for your memory, so the very old and very young might have fun with it. Give each player a pad and pencil and have them tear sheets of paper into roughly the size of playing cards. Take turns going through *So to Speak* to find "pairs" of expressions—expressions that have at least one word in common. (**The devil is in the details** and **speak of the devil** are a pair; so are **the apple of my eye** and **the eye of the storm**.) When a player finds a pair, they should write down each expression on its own card. Once the group has sixteen completed playing cards (that's eight pairs of expressions), shuffle all the cards and lay them facedown in a four-by-four grid on a table. Each player then takes a turn flipping two cards at once; a player gets to keep the cards if they uncover a pair, plus gets to flip another two cards as a reward. As soon as they don't get a match, their turn is over. (Players can get better as the game goes on by trying to memorize the grid.) Continue until there are no cards left on the grid. Whoever has the most cards wins.

20. DRAWING A BLANK.

Choose one player to be emcee, hand them *So to Speak*, and let them scan the book to find a bunch of expressions that contain the same word. (Let's say they pick the word *mad*.) Have them silently pick just one expression as their secret choice (let's say they choose **a mad dash**), then have them announce the word (*mad*) to the group. Go around the circle, letting each player guess the secret expression. (Maybe players make good—but wrong!—guesses, like **mad money**, **mad as hell**, and **madman**.) Keep going until a player guesses right. Give a point to that player, and give the emcee a point for each wrong guess during the round. After everyone has a turn as emcee, the player with the most points wins.

21. MY MAMA TOLD ME.

Pass out pencils and paper and for five minutes have each player write down phrases that their elders—parents, teachers, grandparents, other relatives—use regularly, or used growing up. Next, go around the circle sharing these expressions, and have the group guess what each one means. If the group doesn't know a certain expression, the player who thought of it can share its meaning. After all the expressions are shared and discussed, look at the last category of *So to Speak*—"Our Favorite Family Expressions & Nana-isms"—to see if any of your family expressions match ours. (If so, maybe we hail from the same side of the tracks.) This one's also a great litmus test for couples who are getting to know each other!

22. PARTS OF SPEECH.

Give each player a pencil, a pad of paper, and a copy of *So to Speak*. (If you only have one copy, put it in the center of the table and share.) Choose one player to be emcee and have them pick any word and announce it to the group. (Let's say they choose *intelligent*.) Set a timer for five minutes and have the other players try to think of three different expressions (using *So to Speak* as a resource) that describe the emcee's chosen word—with one big catch: one expression has to be a noun (or noun phrase), one has to be a verb (or verb phrase), and one has to be an adjective (or adjective phrase). To match *intelligent*, for instance, someone might write **a smart cookie** (noun), **firing on all cylinders** (verb), and **smart as a whip** (adjective). Players who come up with all three parts of speech before the timer goes off get one point. Keep playing until someone gets three points. (If you want an easier version of this game, just pick one part of speech, like nouns/noun phrases.)

23. GUESS MY CATEGORY.

Time to go in reverse. Put players into two teams and have one player from each team go head-to-head against each other. Have these players turn to a page in *So to Speak*, keeping it a secret which category they're in. (Let's say they choose the "Sleep & Dreams" category.) This is when it gets a little tricky: Have Player A read one expression aloud from the chosen page, after which Team B—the *other* team—has a chance to guess the category. (So, Player A should try to choose an expression that *doesn't* give the category away; maybe they choose **let sleeping dogs lie**, and Team B wrongly guesses the "Animals" category.) If Team B is unable to guess the category, have Player B read a different expression aloud from the chosen page and give Team A the chance to guess the category. The first team to guess the category correctly wins the round. Keep playing, switching which team goes first each round, until one team wins five rounds. (If you need some help with this one, consult the table of contents to see the full list of categories.)

24. MATCHMAKER.

Give each player a pencil and a pad, and have all players silently write down five subjects (names, places, or things) on a piece of paper. Then cut up the pieces of paper so each item is on its own strip and pile all the subject strips in a bowl. Next, pass *So to Speak* around the group and let each player write down ten expressions from the book (making sure to choose a variety of expressions). Then have each player cut the expressions into strips and hold on to their pile. Choose a judge and have them pick one subject strip from the bowl and read it aloud—let's say it says "Bill Gates." Each player then chooses one expression strip that best fits the subject—maybe **sharp as a tack**, **a whiz kid**, or **a bookworm**—and passes it to the judge facedown (so they can't tell which expression came from which player). Once everyone has handed over their strip, the judge mixes them up and reads them out loud, then chooses their favorite to determine the winner of the round. The winner gets the subject strip as a prize. After you play seven rounds, using a new judge for each round, the player with the most subject strips wins!

25. EAT YOUR WORDS.

This real-life cooking challenge is a different **kettle of fish** indeed—and less a competition than a fun culinary learning experience, especially for parents and little kids together. Open *So to Speak* to the "Food & Cooking" category and put together a three-course meal with an expression paired to each course. Start with an appetizer (**soup's on**, perhaps?), move on to the entrée (make sure to **use your noodl**e when cooking spaghetti), and to finish up? Maybe it's time to **let them eat cake** after all.

BONUS GAME: NEEDLES ALL OVER.

You're only allowed to play this game after playing every other game in this section, as it requires knowing *So to Speak* inside out. We hid one very special expression, **like finding a needle in a haystack**, in seven places throughout *So to Speak*, including where it rightly belongs (in the "Farm" category). Can you find all seven instances? (If you do, head to our website, SoToSpeakBook.com, to let us know!)

A knight in shining armor

THE
EXPRESSIONS

Can you guess the expression each picture represents?

1. *Buffaloed*   2. *The lion's share*   3. *Play cat and mouse*   4. *At a snail's pace*

ANIMALS

- Clam up
- Happy as a clam
- An old crab
- Crabby
- Slippery as an eel
- A big fish in a small pond
- Bigger fish to fry
- Catching the big fish

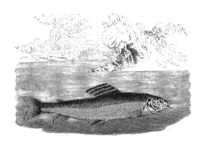

A big fish in a small pond

- A cold fish
- He drinks like a fish
- A fine kettle of fish
- A fish out of water
- Like a fish to water
- Go fish
- Gone fishin'
- Neither fish nor fowl
- Only dead fish go with the flow
- Other fish to fry
- Plenty of fish in the sea
- Live in a fishbowl
- A fishy story
- Something's fishy

- A fluke win
- Stuffed to the gills
- Holy mackerel!
- Like a salmon
- Packed in like sardines
- Jump the shark
- Keep the sharks at bay
- The sharks are circling
- Swimming with sharks
- Come out of your shell
- A shell of himself
- Shell out
- Withdraw into your own shell
- A shellback
- A whale of a time
- Bear a grudge
- A bear hug
- Bear the brunt
- Bear with me

A bear hug

Bear with me

- Bear witness
- Bring to bear
- Can't bear to think about it
- Gruff as a bear
- Lose your bearings
- Be bearish
- Bad news bears
- Buffaloed
- The straw that broke the camel's back
- Get over the hump
- Hump day
- An alley cat
- Bell the cat
- A cat burglar
- Cat got your tongue?
- Cat nap
- Like a cat on a hot tin roof
- Like a cat on hot bricks
- Cat's cradle
- A cool cat
- A copycat
- A copycat crime
- Curiosity killed the cat

- A dead-cat bounce
- A fat cat
- Grin like a Cheshire cat
- Let the cat out of the bag
- Look what the cat dragged in
- Nervous as a cat having kittens
- Not enough room to swing a cat
- Play cat and mouse
- A scaredy-cat
- There's more than one way to skin a cat
- Walk the cat back
- The cat's meow
- The cat's pajamas
- When the cat's away . . .
- Fight like cats and dogs
- Like herding cats
- Raining cats and dogs
- Catty-corner
- Feeling frisky
- Cute as a kitten
- Weak as a kitten
- Dip into the kitty
- Feed the kitty
- A leopard never changes its spots
- Brave as a lion
- Lionhearted
- In like a lion, out like a lamb
- The lion's share

A scaredy-cat

- Twist the lion's tail
- Walk into the lion's den
- Lionize
- Throw to the lions
- Pussyfoot around
- The roaring '20s
- Easy, tiger
- A paper tiger
- Have a tiger by the tail
- A tiger can't change its stripes
- A tiger mother
- Gee whiskers!
- A deer in the headlights
- Swift as a deer
- Go stag
- A stag party
- Bark at someone

- Bark at the moon
- His bark is worse than his bite
- Bulldog determination
- Attack dog
- A dog and pony show
- The dog days of summer
- A dog in the manger
- Dog someone
- Dog tired
- A dog whistle
- Like a dog with a bone
- That dog won't hunt
- Dog years
- Dog-eared pages
- A dog-eat-dog world
- A dogfight
- Every dog has its day
- A hangdog look

Put on the dog

- Have no dog in this fight
- A lap dog
- Meaner than a junkyard dog
- Put on the dog
- A shaggy-dog story

- Sick as a dog
- The tail wagging the dog
- The top dog
- Treat like a dog
- The underdog
- Wag the dog
- Crooked as a dog's hind leg
- In a dog's age
- A dog's breakfast
- A dog's day
- A dog's life
- Not a dog's chance
- Dogged pursuit
- A doggie bag
- A doggone shame
- In the doghouse
- Barking dogs seldom bite
- My dogs are barking
- Crazy like a fox
- He's a fox
- Like a fox guarding the henhouse
- A fox in the chicken coop

- Sly as a fox
- Outfoxed
- Foxy lady
- To hound
- Clean as a hound's tooth
- Keep on a short leash
- Strain at the leash
- Put a muzzle on it
- Ahead of the pack
- Leader of the pack
- Pull away from the pack
- Puppy love
- A big bad wolf
- Cry wolf
- Hold the wolf by the ears
- Keep the wolf from the door
- A lone wolf
- A wolf in sheep's clothing
- Wolf down
- A wolf whistle

A snake in the grass

- Keep the wolves at bay
- Throw to the wolves
- Ferret out
- A mole in the organization
- Weasel words
- Weasel your way out of it
- Lying weasels
- Alligator arms
- Crocodile tears
- A frog in the throat
- Leapfrog over
- Finer than a frog's hair
- A lounge lizard
- Boo, hiss!
- Mean as a rattlesnake
- Roll snake eyes
- Slippery as a snake
- A snake in the grass
- Snake in one's bosom
- A snake oil salesman
- A snake pit

Crocodile tears

- Snake the drain
- Snake through
- Toady up to someone
- Slow as a turtle
- Turn turtle
- Off like a herd of turtles
- A kangaroo court
- Tie your shoe, kangaroo
- Buck naked
- Buck the system
- Buck the tide
- Buck tradition
- Buck up
- Buck wild

Be bullish

- Like a bull in a china shop
- Cut through the bull
- To hit the bull's-eye
- That's no bull
- Strong as a bull

- Take the bull by the horns
- Bullheaded
- Be bullish
- The bulls and bears of Wall Street
- Kill the fatted calf
- A cattle call
- Packed in like cattle
- Don't have a cow
- Cowed into submission
- Till the cows come home
- He's a donkey
- Donkey's years
- Get fleeced
- Get your goat
- An old goat
- A scapegoat
- Hide behind something
- Tan your hide
- Go hog wild
- Go whole hog
- Hog the limelight
- Hog-tie someone
- In hog heaven
- Call hogs
- It's hogwash
- Don't put the cart before the horse
- Get back on the horse
- A hobbyhorse
- A horse-and-buggy solution

- Horse and rabbit stew
- Horsefeathers
- The horse has left the barn
- A horse of a different color
- It's a horse race
- Horse sense

A horse's ass

- Horse-trade
- Horseplay
- Horses for courses
- Lock the stable door after the horse has bolted
- A horse's ass
- Change horses midstream
- Wild horses couldn't drag me away
- Be a workhorse
- Horse around
- Feel like a jackass

Pig out

- Innocent as a lamb
- Like a lamb to the slaughter
- Meek as a lamb
- In two shakes of a lamb's tail
- Stubborn as a mule
- Strong as an ox
- Fat as a pig
- Happy as a pig in mud
- A pig in a poke
- Pig out
- Pigheaded
- A selfish pig
- Like a stuffed pig
- In a pig's eye
- Piggyback on
- When pigs fly
- Pony up
- Free rein
- Keep a tight rein on something

- Rein something in
- Pull in the reins
- Take the reins
- Always saddle your own horse
- Back in the saddle
- A burr under your saddle
- Saddle up
- Be saddled with
- Be sheepish
- Cast your pearls before swine
- Badger the witness
- He's a honey badger
- Quit badgering me!
- Busy as a beaver
- An eager beaver
- Cute as a bunny
- Quick as a bunny
- Use as a guinea pig

- Be on a hamster wheel
- A harebrained scheme
- The best-laid plans of mice and men
- Quiet as a mouse
- Down the rabbit hole
- Pull a rabbit out of a hat
- A rabbit punch
- A dirty rat
- Rat around
- Rat on someone
- The rat race
- Like rats deserting a sinking ship
- The skunk at the garden party
- Get skunked
- Squirrel away

Pull in the reins

- Slug it out
- Slow as a snail
- Snail mail
- At a snail's pace
- The elephant in the room
- A memory like an elephant
- A grease monkey
- Make a monkey out of
- Monkey around
- Monkey bars
- Monkey business
- Like a monkey doing a math problem
- Monkey in the middle
- A monkey on your back
- Monkey see, monkey do
- Throw a monkey wrench into
- I'll be a monkey's uncle
- A zebra can't change its stripes
- No such animal
- A party animal
- A whole different animal
- A beast of burden
- True bred
- Rattle someone's cage
- A creature of habit
- Make the fur fly
- Cull the herd
- Herd mentality
- Horn in on something

A monkey on your back

- Hornswoggle
- On the horns of a dilemma
- Lock horns with
- Pull in your horns
- The pick of the litter
- The runt of the litter
- A pet peeve
- A pet project
- Something preying on your mind
- In the clutches of
- Bust your tail
- Drag your tail
- Give up and turn tail

- Hightail it out of there
- Kick some tail
- Leave with your tail between your legs
- On his tail
- At the tail end
- Tail someone
- Go into a tailspin
- A wild hunch
- A wild imagination

AROUND THE WORLD

1. _Like a Greek goddess_ 2. _To go Dutch_

Storm the Bastille

- Only in America
- American as apple pie
- The American dream
- An American icon
- The Arab spring
- Atlantis
- Clean the Augean stables
- Storm the Bastille
- The Big Apple
- Kiss the Blarney Stone

- The toast of Broadway
- A Bronx cheer
- You can take the boy out of the Bronx, but you can't take the Bronx out of the boy
- Sell the Brooklyn Bridge
- Shuffle off to Buffalo
- A slow boat to China
- Cardboard city
- The city of bridges
- The City of Brotherly Love

- The city of lights
- The city that never sleeps
- A city slicker
- The Emerald City
- The Emerald Isle
- The Eternal City
- The Motor City
- Tent city
- The Miracle of Coogan's Bluff
- Send to Coventry

- A road-to-Damascus moment
- Something is rotten in the state of Denmark
- Go Dutch
- Dutch treat
- Dutch uncle

Fancy meeting you here

- Get your Dutch up
- The garden of Eden
- Seeking El Dorado
- French kiss
- Geographically undesirable
- A Georgia peach
- Solid as the Rock of Gibraltar
- Think globally, act locally
- Like a Greek goddess
- It's Greek to me

- A modern-day Greek tragedy
- Go to Halifax
- A Hollywood ending
- The fighting Irish
- Get your Irish up
- We're not in Kansas anymore
- Fancy meeting you here
- There's no joy in Mudville
- In a New York minute
- New York state of mind
- Coals to Newcastle
- True North
- Remember Pearl Harbor
- Remember the Alamo
- Remember the *Maine*
- Putting on the Ritz
- All roads lead to Rome
- Rome wasn't built in a day
- Skid row
- Play Russian roulette
- Shangri-La
- Sent to Siberia
- A bellwether state
- The Empire State
- A fugue state
- The Garden State
- A state of flux
- The state of play
- The Sunshine State

- It's like Grand Central Station in here
- From Wall Street to Main Street
- Occupy Wall Street
- Take a bath on Wall Street
- All the way to Timbuktu
- It's all over town
- Hit the town
- Toast of the town
- A Trojan horse
- Work like a Trojan
- What happens in Vegas stays in Vegas
- It takes a village
- The Washington establishment
- Meet one's Waterloo
- The Great White Way
- The wild West

Rome wasn't built in a day

ARTS & ENTERTAINMENT

1.

1. Toot your own horn 2. March to the beat of your own drum 3. Act the fool

- Act as if there's no tomorrow
- Act high and mighty
- Act like a child
- Act like you're above something
- Act out
- Act superior
- Act the fool

A balancing act

- Act up
- Act your age
- A balancing act
- Caught in the act
- Clean up your act
- A disappearing act
- Act the part
- The final act
- Get into the act
- Get your act together
- A juggling act
- An opening act

- Polish your act
- Put on an act
- A tough act to follow
- A bad actor
- Worth the price of admission
- Drop an album
- The art of overlooking
- The art of the deal
- Have it down to an art
- Master the art of
- State of the art
- A budding artist
- A choke artist
- A con artist
- An escape artist
- A tortured artist
- Artistic license
- An audience of one
- A captive audience
- Beat the band
- Get the band back together
- Strike up the band
- Bang on
- Start with a bang
- A banger
- The beat goes on
- Beat the rap
- Beats me
- He doesn't miss a beat
- Be offbeat

- Take a beating
- All the bells and whistles
- Get your bell rung
- That rings a bell
- Saved by the bell
- I'll be there with bells on
- Get top billing
- Bow out
- Broad strokes
- Brush up
- A brush with greatness
- Bugle call
- The camera adds ten pounds
- On camera
- Cast aspersions
- Chime in
- Hit the right chord
- Strike a chord

That rings a bell

- Make a circus out of
- Like a three-ring circus
- He's a clown
- Clown around

Dance with the devil

- Send in the clowns
- Clap back
- On a roller coaster
- A comedy of errors
- Right on cue
- Take a cue from someone
- Behind the curtain
- Bring down the curtain
- A curtain call
- A curtain raiser
- Curtains up
- Dance around an issue
- My dance card is full
- Dance like no one is watching
- Dance on your grave
- Dance with the devil
- By accident or design
- Put on display
- Closet drama

- A drama queen
- A flair for the dramatic
- Beat to the draw
- Draw a blank
- Draw to a close
- Draw a conclusion
- Draw a line in the sand
- Draw attention
- Draw down
- Draw first blood
- Draw from
- Draw him out
- Draw straws
- Draw the short straw
- Back to the drawing board
- Know where to draw a line
- Quick on the draw

Quick on the draw

- Slow and easy on the draw
- A drawback
- Beat your own drum
- A drum major instinct

Fiddling around

- Drum up
- Drum up business
- March to a different drummer
- March to the beat of your own drum
- Tight as a drum
- Get an encore
- Make a grand entrance
- Head for the exits
- Make a grand exit
- A claim to fame
- Play someone like a fiddle
- Fiddling around
- Flaunt it
- Out of focus
- Be unfocused
- Not my forte
- I was framed
- The right frame of mind
- Front and center
- Play to the gallery
- In the groove
- Feeling groovy
- In the guise of

- Take on many guises
- Air guitar
- Harp on
- A mouth harp
- Toot your own horn
- And all that jazz
- Jazz it up
- Jazzed up
- The jig is up
- Juggle many balls in the air
- Like juggling sand
- Low-key
- Sing off-key
- A tight-knit group
- Stick to your knitting
- Wax lyrical
- Work your magic
- Drop the mic
- Bust a move
- Music charms the savage breast
- That's music to my ears
- Play musical chairs
- End on a sour note
- A false note
- Find the right note
- Hit a high note
- On that note
- Sound a sour note
- Turn into a soap opera
- Orchestrate

- In the paint
- Paint the town
- Paint yourself into a corner
- Paint with a broad brush
- A bit part
- A good part
- Have a part in something
- Look the part
- Part with
- The good parts
- A command performance
- A repeat performance

Harp on

- A photographic memory
- He's in the picture
- A mixed picture
- Out of the picture

- A picture is worth a thousand words
- Picture perfect
- Picture this
- Pretty as a picture
- Pitch perfect
- Pose a challenge
- The poster boy for
- Give props
- Break a record
- Get something on the record
- Off the record
- On the record
- For the record
- The record speaks for itself
- Set the record straight
- Sound like a broken record
- It doesn't ring a bell
- It doesn't ring true
- Ring in the new year
- It rings hollow
- Let's rock and roll
- Burst onto the scene
- Make a scene
- It's a mob scene
- A change of scenery
- Behind the scenes
- Flip the script
- On the edge of your seat
- A front-row seat

Get into the swing of things

- A sellout
- All show and no go
- A feel-good show
- Get the show on the road
- The greatest show on earth
- Hold down the show
- He's a show horse, not a workhorse
- The show must go on
- Show off
- Show your stuff
- A sideshow
- A strong showing
- A showstopper
- Sing a different tune
- Sing for your supper
- Sing his praises
- Sing Kumbaya
- Sing the blues
- Be sketchy
- A sketchy neighborhood
- A sold-out crowd
- A fight song

- The same old song and dance
- A sounding board for
- In the spotlight
- A squeeze box
- All the world's a stage
- A new stage of life
- Set the stage
- Stage fright
- Stage left
- Stage right
- Take center stage
- Upstaged
- Steal the show
- Steal the spotlight
- Another string to your bow
- Able to swing it
- Get into the swing of things
- Back in full swing
- Swing a certain way
- Swing by
- Variations on a theme
- That's the ticket
- Tickle the ivories
- Change your tone
- Set the tone
- Tone it down
- To use a harsh tone
- Up to your old tricks
- A real trouper
- Belt out a tune

- Call the tune
- Carry a tune
- Change your tune
- Out of tune
- Play your tune
- Tune something out
- Stay tuned
- Tuned in
- Fine tuning
- Usher into place
- Waltz through life
- Not just whistling Dixie

Back in full swing

ASTRONOMY

Reach for the moon

Over the moon

- On the horizon
- Broaden your horizons
- Ask for the moon
- A blood moon
- Gone between the moon and the milkman
- The moon on a stick
- Moon over someone
- Moon someone
- Over the moon
- Promise the moon
- Reach for the moon
- Shoot for the moon
- Shoot the moon
- He thinks she hung the moon and stars

- Moonlight
- Many moons ago
- Moonstruck
- Waxing and waning
- On a different planet
- From another planet
- Sky high
- The sky is falling
- The sky's the limit
- Lost in space
- A space cadet
- Space out
- Spacey
- A rising star
- She's a shining star
- Star-crossed lovers
- Wish upon a star
- Reach for the stars
- Shoot for the stars
- When the stars align
- Ask for the sun and the moon
- Bask in the sun
- Your day in the sun
- Everything under the sun
- The land of the rising sun
- Moment in the sun
- Never let the sun go down on your anger
- Nothing new under the sun
- Soak up the sun

The Sunbelt

- The Sunbelt

- Sun worshipper

- He thinks the sun rises and sets on him

- Sun's out, guns out

- Approaching your sunset years

- Ride off into the sunset

- A sunset provision

Sun worshipper

AUTOMOTIVE

1.

2.

- Hit the brakes
- Pump the brakes
- Put on the brakes
- Slam on the brakes
- Bumper-to-bumper traffic
- Throw someone under the bus
- Getaway car
- Be clutch
- Come through in the clutch
- On a collision course
- The course of the day
- The course of life
- A crash course
- Stay the course
- Firing on all cylinders
- Put the top-down
- Drive away
- Drive home your point
- Drive off

- Drive someone up the wall
- Drive up
- In overdrive
- Test-drive
- Be driven
- Driven crazy
- Driven mad
- Driven up a pole
- A backseat driver
- In the driver's seat
- Driving me to drink
- Rev the engine
- Soup up the engine
- A fender bender
- It's a gas
- Pass gas
- Run out of gas
- Step on the gas
- Gear up

- Get yourself in gear
- In high gear
- Kick into high gear
- Shift gears
- Switch gears

Get hitched

- That really grinds my gears
- Throwing sand in the gears
- Grease the skids
- Grease the wheels
- Come to a screeching halt
- Come to a grinding halt
- Get hitched
- Look under the hood
- Get jacked
- A limousine liberal
- To see it in the rearview mirror
- A motorhead
- A motormouth

Driven up a pole

- Spare parts
- Backpedal
- Put the pedal to the metal
- To soft-pedal something
- A drag race
- A slow ride
- Take for a ride
- Go joyriding
- There's a lot riding on it
- Ride shotgun
- Run smoothly
- Running on empty
- Running on fumes
- Rust out
- A spark in one's eye
- A spark of an idea
- Sparks flying
- Get up to speed
- Pick up speed
- Up to speed
- Take it out for a spin
- By fits and starts
- Kick-start something
- Steer clear
- To steer someone wrong
- A pit stop
- Have a spare tire
- Kick the tires
- Built like a Mack truck
- Have no truck with

Take the wheel

- Keep on truckin'
- Get a tune-up
- Make a U-turn
- Don't know where to turn
- Take a left turn
- Take a sharp turn
- Turn something around
- Behind the wheel
- A big wheel
- Reinventing the wheel
- Take the wheel
- Wheel and deal
- A wheeler-dealer
- Spinning your wheels
- The wheels are coming off
- The wheels are spinning

BEVERAGES

1. Put a cork in it   2. Raise a glass to someone   3. Good to the last drop

- A beer belly
- Beer goggles
- Cry in your beer
- One beer short of a six-pack
- Hit the bottle
- Bottled up
- To cap it all off
- Put a cap on something
- Crack open the champagne
- Champagne taste on a beer budge
- Coffee klatch
- Coffee talk
- You're the cream in my coffee
- Put a cork in it
- A corker
- My cup runneth over
- You can't pour from an empty cup
- Drink it in
- Drinking age
- Like drinking from a fire hose
- Drunk as a skunk
- Drunk with power
- Under the influence
- Good to the last drop
- A glass is half-full or half-empty
- Raise a glass to someone
- The juice is worth the squeeze
- Run out of juice
- Get the creative juices flowing

- Stew in your own juices
- A juicy detail
- Drink the Kool-Aid
- Like a fly in milk
- The land of milk and honey
- Milk it for all it's worth
- Milk the bull
- Like milking a duck
- A pub crawl
- Pleased as punch
- Take away the punch bowl
- Sober as a priest
- Sober as a judge
- Sober up
- A sobering thought
- A soda jerk

- On tap
- Tap out
- High tea
- Not my cup of tea
- Read the tea leaves
- Spill the tea
- Tea and sympathy
- Quench your thirst
- A thirst for knowledge
- A thirst for life
- Aged like fine wine
- Like old wine in new bottles
- Wine and dine someone

Bottled up

BIG & SMALL

A big head

Too big to fail

- Big as a barn
- Big as a house
- Big as all outdoors
- Big data
- The big easy
- A big gun
- A big head
- A big hit
- The big kahuna
- Big man on campus
- Be big on something
- A big person
- A big stick
- A big talker
- A big-ticket item
- Big time
- A big to-do
- Bring out the big guns
- Go big or go home
- Make a big splash
- Make it big
- See the big picture
- Think big
- Too big to fail
- Under the big top

- What's the big idea?
- Of epic proportions
- By and large
- Bits and pieces
- Downsize
- The lesser of two evils
- A little birdie told me
- A little bit at a time
- Little ol' me
- Of little import
- Too little, too late

- Small as a mustard seed
- Make small talk
- No small wonder
- A small fry
- A small town feel
- It's a small world
- A small-timer

Make small talk

BIRDS, BATS & INSECTS

1. A social butterfly 2. A gone goose 3. Wise as an owl

- Like a bat out of hell
- Blind as a bat
- He didn't bat an eye
- Bats in the belfry
- An albatross around your neck
- Wet your beak
- A bird-brained idea
- Bird-dogging
- Flip the bird
- Have a bird's-eye view
- In the catbird seat
- Naked as a jaybird
- He's a rare bird
- A strange bird
- A tough old bird
- A birdbrain
- Birds of a feather
- Charm the birds from the trees
- Lovebirds
- Snowbirds
- That's strictly for the birds
- The canary in the coal mine
- Sing like a canary
- A chick flick
- My little chickadee
- A chicken in every pot
- A chicken-or-egg situation
- Chicken out
- Chicken scratch
- Chickenhearted

Snowbirds

- Chicken-livered
- Like a chicken playing chess
- That's not chicken feed
- The chickens are coming home to roost
- Go to bed with the chickens
- Fly the coop
- Cooped up
- Stick in your craw
- As the crow flies
- Something to crow about
- A crow's nest
- My turtle dove
- Dovetail nicely with
- Dovish

- Duck and cover
- Duck out
- Duck the issue
- If it walks like a duck
- It's duck soup
- Lucky duck
- Odd duck
- A sitting duck
- Take to something like a duck to water
- Water off a duck's back
- Ugly duckling
- Ducks on the pond
- Get your ducks in a row
- Bald as an eagle
- An eagle eye
- The eagle has landed
- A feather in your cap
- Feather your nest
- Knock me over with a feather
- Shake your tail feather
- Show the white feather

Get your ducks in a row

- Soft as down feathers
- Fine-feathered friend
- Ruffle some feathers
- Stray from the flock
- Take a gander
- The golden goose
- A gone goose
- Goose bumps
- Your goose is cooked
- The goose that laid the golden egg

Fine-feathered friend

- Lay a goose egg
- Loose as a goose
- A wild goose chase
- Silly as a goose
- What's good for the goose . . .
- Wouldn't say boo to a goose
- Raise one's hackles

- In the booby hatch
- Hawkish
- A hen party
- Henpecked
- Mad as a wet hen
- A mother hen
- An old hen
- Rare as hen's teeth
- Give a hoot
- Hoot and holler
- You're a hoot!
- Happy as a lark
- On a lark
- Build a nest egg
- Foul one's own nest
- Leave the nest
- An empty-nester
- An ostrich defense
- The ostrich generation
- A night owl
- Wise as an owl
- To parrot
- Proud as a peacock
- Peckish
- A stool pigeon
- Pigeonhole
- A round-robin tournament
- Rule the roost
- Do a swan dive
- Graceful as a swan

Talk turkey

- Swan song
- A real turkey
- Stuffed like a turkey
- Talk turkey
- A turkey
- The vultures are circling
- On a wing and a prayer
- Take under his wing
- Winging it
- A chance to spread your wings
- Clip his wings
- Earn your wings
- Waiting in the wings
- Feeling antsy
- A bee in your bonnet
- Busy as a bee
- A worker bee
- Make a beeline for
- Like bees to honey
- Mind your own beeswax
- The birds and the bees
- Get the bug

- Bug a home
- A bug in the system
- Bug off
- Bug out
- Bug someone
- Bug-eyed
- Crazy as a bedbug
- Debug
- Put a bug in your ear
- Cute as a bug's ear
- What's bugging you?
- Butterflies in your stomach
- A social butterfly
- Hear crickets
- A flea market
- Happy as a flea in a doghouse
- They're dropping like flies
- It flies in the face of logic
- There are no flies on him
- Be fly
- A fly in the ointment
- A fly on the wall
- A fly-by-night operation
- A gadfly
- Goodbye, housefly
- It'll never fly
- On the fly
- She wouldn't hurt a fly
- Working on the fly
- Knee-high to a grasshopper

- Mad as a hornet
- Open up a hornet's nest
- Nitpick
- A pest
- Cross-pollinate
- Conduct a sting operation
- Take the sting out of it
- Tick it off
- Ticked off
- Search the web
- Spin a web of lies
- Web of deceit
- What a tangled web we weave
- Try to wiggle your way out
  of something
- Be a worm
- The worm has turned
- Worm your way out of

Conduct a sting operation

BOATING

Paddle your own canoe

- Anchors aweigh
- Aye-aye, captain
- Bail out
- Above board

Aye-aye, captain

- Go overboard
- On board
- Don't rock the boat
- In the same boat
- Miss the boat
- Showboat
- Swift-boat someone
- Lower the boom
- On cruise control
- A shakedown cruise
- You're cruisin' for a bruisin'
- Hit the deck
- On deck
- Like rearranging the deck chairs on the *Titanic*
- Clear the decks
- In the doldrums

- Float a loan
- Float an idea
- Keep it afloat
- Whatever floats your boat
- Flotsam and jetsam
- Packed to the gunwales
- Safe harbor
- Down the hatch
- Batten down the hatches
- Into a strong headwind
- At the helm
- Even keel
- Keel over
- Spring a leak
- Thrown a line
- Nail your colors to the mast
- Have just one oar in the water
- Don't rest on your oars
- Paddle upstream
- Paddle your own canoe
- The last port of call
- Throw a life preserver
- Make a row
- Row upstream
- Sail close to the wind
- Sail off into the sunset
- Sail on
- Sail right through
- Sail through rough seas
- Sail under false colors

- Clear sailing
- Smooth sailing
- A mouth like a sailor
- Trim your sails
- At sea
- Lost at sea
- A sea change
- Sea legs
- Abandon ship
- Captain the ship
- Don't give up the ship
- Go down with the ship
- Jump ship
- Right the ship
- Run a tight ship
- The ship has sailed
- Ship him off
- It's a sinking ship
- Steer the ship of state
- Waiting for my ship to come in
- Like ships passing in the night

Down the hatch

A sinking feeling

- Everything's shipshape
- Shipwrecked
- A sinking feeling
- Full steam ahead
- A bum steer
- From stem to stern
- Made of sterner stuff
- Wade through something
- In the wake of
- In your wheelhouse

BODY

1. Long in the tooth 2. On the one hand 3. Kick up your heels 4. Put your finger on something

- Bite on something
- Bite someone's head off
- Okay, I'll bite
- A biting sense of humor
- In the blink of an eye
- Who will blink first?
- A brain dump
- A brain fart
- Brain food
- Brain freeze
- Brain power
- A brain teaser
- A brain trust
- Something on the brain

Pick someone's brain

- Mommy brain
- Pick someone's brain
- Left-brained
- Right-brained
- It's a no-brainer

- The brains of the operation
- Brains vs. Brawn
- Don't beat your brains out
- Have no brains
- Knock your brains out
- Wrack your brain
- Brainstorm
- Form a brain trust
- Brainwashed
- Browbeat someone
- Highbrow
- Lowbrow
- Raise eyebrows
- Turn the other cheek
- Cheeky
- Chin music
- Don't stick your chin out
- Keep your chin up
- Lead with your chin
- Take it on the chin
- All choked up
- Choked with emotion
- Bust someone's chops
- Lick your chops
- Prove your chops
- For crying out loud!
- Bend my ear
- Chew his ear off
- Ear worm
- A tin ear

- Have his ear
- In one ear and out the other
- Keep an ear out
- Out on his ear

All ears

- Play it by ear
- Pull in your ear
- Turned on its ear
- Get an earful
- Earmark
- All ears
- Can't believe my ears
- My ears are burning
- His ears perked up
- I'm going to have my ears lowered
- Coming out of your ears
- Nothing between the ears
- Keep your ears open
- Lend me your ears
- Pin someone's ears back
- Tune out your ears
- Up to my ears in
- Wet behind the ears

- Within earshot
- Catch some shut-eye
- It caught my eye
- The evil eye
- Eye candy
- An eye for an eye
- The eye of the storm
- The eye of the tiger
- An eye-catcher
- An eye-opener
- An eye-opening experience
- An eyesore
- As far as the eye can see
- Get an eyeful
- I'd give my eyeteeth
- Give the stink eye
- Have an eye for value
- Live in the public eye
- Keep a close eye on
- Keep a watchful eye
- Keep an eye on it
- Keep an eye out
- Keep your eye on the ball
- Look him in the eye
- There's more to it than meets the eye
- Not a dry eye in the house
- It's a poke in the eye
- A roving eye
- See eye to eye

- It struck my eye
- Turn a blind eye
- Turn a wary eye to
- Unfold before your very eyes
- Eyeball something
- Up to your eyeballs
- Wide-eyed
- Bat your eyelashes
- Close your eyes to

Keep your eye on the ball

- Cry your eyes out
- Cut eyes at
- Do something with your eyes closed

- Easy on the eyes
- His eyes light up
- Eyes on the prize
- Your eyes will pop
- For your eyes only
- A fresh pair of eyes
- All eyes on something
- Both eyes open
- Eyes in the back of your head
- Have eyes on
- The scales fall from your eyes
- Right between the eyes
- Keep your eyes peeled
- Make eyes at someone
- Poke his eyes out
- Roll your eyes
- Spit in your eye
- A treat for the eyes
- Bawl your eyes out
- Bawl out
- A cockeyed optimist
- A blank look on your face
- An about-face
- Facedown
- A face for radio
- A face in the crowd
- A face like thunder
- Face off
- A face only a mother could love
- Face the music

Face to face

- Face to face
- Face up to it
- A face-lift
- A face-off
- Fall flat on your face
- Get some face time
- In your face!
- Lose face
- On the face of it
- The public face
- Put a face to the name
- Put a good face on it
- Put on a brave face
- Put on a happy face
- Put on your best face
- Save face
- Show your face
- A slap in the face
- Stuff your face
- Take it at face value
- Get up in someone's face
- What's-his-face
- Why the long face?

- Bald-faced lie
- Forget about it!
- All but forgotten
- Frowned upon
- Gobsmacked
- Grin and bear it
- Gum up the works
- Bad hair day
- Don't set your hair on fire
- Get out of my hair
- Good hair day
- A hair in the butter
- Hair of the dog
- A hair-raiser
- A hairpin turn
- Hanging by a hair
- Let your hair down
- It'll make your hair curl
- It'll make your hair stand on end
- No hair on my tongue
- Like pulling hair

Good hair day

- Raise the hair on your arms
- Saved by a hair
- Tear your hair out
- By a hair's breadth
- Take a haircut
- Hairline fracture
- Split hairs

Things will get hairy

- Hairy at the heel
- Things will get hairy
- It's all in your head
- Like banging your head against a wall
- Bring it to a head
- Bury your head in the sand
- Call for his head
- I can't wrap my head around it
- Come to a head
- Confront it head-on
- From head to toe

- Get a head start
- Go over someone's head
- Go to the head of the class
- Go to your head
- Have a good head on your shoulders
- Have a head for business
- Have something hanging over your head
- Have your head examined
- Have your head handed to you
- Have your head on straight
- Have your head screwed on right
- Have your head served up on a platter
- Head and shoulders above the rest
- A head count
- Head down
- Headfirst
- Head honcho
- His head is on the block
- The head of household
- Head of state
- Head off
- Head off at the pass
- Head out
- Head over heels
- A head-to-toe examination
- Head up
- A head-on collision

- To be hit over the head with
- In over your head
- It just popped into my head
- Keep one's head above water
- Keep your head about you
- Lose your head
- It'll make your head spin
- Know your head from a hole in the ground
- Off with his head!
- On one's head
- A pinhead
- Put an idea in your head
- A swelled head

- Heads I win, tails you lose
- Heads up!
- Heads will roll
- Put your heads together
- Headstrong
- Make headway
- By no stretch of the imagination
- Capture your imagination
- It's a figment of your imagination
- An overactive imagination
- A glass jaw
- A jaw-dropping experience
- Out of the jaws of death

Put your heads together

- The titular head
- Touched in the head
- A towhead
- Turn it on its head
- Use your head!
- It went right over his head
- Where's your head?
- Banging heads
- Call heads or tails
- Can't make heads nor tails of it
- Get a heads-up

- Have a good laugh
- Have the last laugh
- Laugh it up
- Laugh out loud
- Laugh your head off
- Laughed out of the room
- Burst out laughing
- It's no laughing matter
- A laughingstock
- Just for laughs
- He's got it licked

- Bite your lip
- Curl your lip
- Don't give me any lip
- Keep a stiff upper lip
- Pay lip service
- Zip your lip
- Tight-lipped
- My lips are sealed
- Loose lips sink ships
- Read my lips
- Do it from memory
- Down the memory hole
- False memory
- Have a short memory
- If memory serves
- Jog one's memory
- Refresh my memory
- Are you out of your mind?
- Bear in mind
- It boggles the mind
- Bored out of my mind
- Change your mind
- Clear your mind
- It didn't cross my mind
- Don't mind if I do
- Fair-minded
- Get your mind out of the gutter
- A dirty mind
- A mind like a sieve
- Have a mind of your own

- In your right mind
- Keep an open mind
- It's a load off my mind
- Lose your mind
- Make up your mind
- A mastermind
- A mind like a steel trap
- Mind over matter
- A mind reader
- Mind the gap
- My mind went blank
- Mind your manners
- Mind-bending
- Mind-boggling
- A mind-meld
- Mind-numbing
- A mindset
- It must've slipped my mind
- It never entered my mind
- Nothing comes to mind
- Of like mind
- Of sound mind
- Peace of mind
- A piece of my mind
- Poison someone's mind
- Presence of mind
- Put your mind at ease
- Put your mind to it
- Speak one's mind
- A state of mind

- To my mind
- It's a weight off my mind
- In my mind's eye
- Closed-minded
- Narrow-minded
- Small-minded
- Tough-minded
- Mindless work
- Great minds think alike
- Little minds
- A meeting of the minds
- Talk out of both sides of your mouth
- Bad-mouth
- A closed mouth
- Don't put words in my mouth
- Foam at the mouth
- From your mouth to god's ears
- Gutter mouth
- Big mouth
- Foul mouth
- It made my mouth water
- Mouth off
- Shut my mouth!
- You took the words right out of my mouth
- Word of mouth
- Close-mouthed
- Mealymouthed
- He said a mouthful
- Serve as a mouthpiece

- Mouths to feed
- Out of the mouths of babes
- Break someone's neck
- Breathing down your neck
- A kink in your neck
- A millstone around your neck
- Move at breakneck speed
- Neck and neck
- Neck with someone
- Risk one's neck
- Save your own neck
- Stick your neck out
- Stiff-necked
- Up to your neck in something
- Wring his neck
- A bloody nose
- Don't get your nose out of joint
- Follow your nose
- Have your nose in the air
- Hit it right on the nose
- Hold your nose
- Keep your nose clean
- Keep your nose out of my business
- Led around by the nose
- Look down your nose at
- Nose above the toes
- Nose blind
- A nose for trouble
- The nose knows

- Nose out
- Nose to the grindstone
- Can't see past the end of your nose
- Plain as the nose on your face
- Poke your nose into something
- It's right under your nose
- Rub his nose in the dirt

Burst into tears

- Snub your nose at
- Turn over on its nose
- Turn up your nose at
- Sitting in the nosebleed section
- Hard-nosed
- Take a nosedive
- To be nosy
- Get it through your thick skull

- Engage in skulduggery
- Crack a smile
- A plastic smile
- That'll put a smile on your face
- Service with a smile
- Smile from ear to ear
- Wipe that smile off your face
- All smiles
- Make a spectacle of yourself
- A spit-take
- Spitball ideas
- Suck it up
- Easy to swallow
- Hard to swallow
- Swallow your pride
- Swallow your words
- Shed a tear over
- A tear-jerker
- Bored to tears
- Burst into tears
- Moved to tears
- Add teeth to it
- Armed to the teeth
- Bare one's teeth
- Clench your teeth
- Cut your teeth on something
- Grit your teeth
- Kick him in the teeth
- I'll knock your teeth out
- Lie through your teeth

- Makes my teeth itch
- It's like pulling teeth
- Show your teeth
- Sink your teeth into it
- Teething troubles
- Cut your own throat
- Cutthroat competition
- Have him by the throat
- Don't jump down my throat
- A lump in your throat
- Ram it down his throat
- Tickle in your throat
- Full-throated
- At each other's throats
- Bite your tongue!
- Get your tongue wagging
- The gift of tongues
- A sharp tongue
- Have your tongue hanging out
- Hold your tongue
- Your mother tongue
- It's on the tip of my tongue
- It rolls off the tongue
- A slip of the tongue
- A still tongue
- Tongue in cheek
- A tongue-lashing
- Tongue-tied
- A tongue-twister
- Believe in the tooth fairy

- Fight tooth and nail
- Long in the tooth
- Put the toothpaste back in the tube
- A toothless wonder

- Toothsome
- A bigwig
- A wink and a nod
- Wink wink, nudge nudge
- Hoodwinked
- No worries
- Put a new wrinkle on it
- Taken aback
- Arm candy
- I'd give my right arm
- The long arm of the law
- On the arm of someone
- Stand arm-in-arm
- Stiff-arm

- Twist my arm
- Strong-arm tactics
- At arm's length
- A call to arms
- Get your arms around it

An arms race

- An arms race
- Lock arms
- Received with open arms
- Take up arms
- Up in arms
- Back away
- Back down
- Back in action
- Back into something
- Back me up
- Back off
- Back out of it
- Back to back
- Back to reality

- Backbreaking work
- Be a backup
- Flat on my back
- Bounce back
- Break my back
- Break the back of
- Cover your back
- With one hand tied behind your back
- Don't hold back
- Get off my back
- Get your back up
- Glad to see the back of him
- We go way back
- I've got your back
- Have your back against the wall
- Knock back
- Leave back
- There's no holding back
- There's no turning back
- Oh, my aching back!
- A pat on the back
- Stabbed in the back
- Suffer a setback
- Take a back seat
- Turn your back on someone
- Watch your back
- No backbiting
- Have no backbone
- It will backfire on you

- Backtrack
- To bend over backward
- You've got it all backward
- Belly laugh
- Into the belly of the beast
- Quit your bellyaching
- Make a clean breast of
- Chest-thumping
- Get it off my chest
- Put hair on your chest
- At one's elbow
- Elbow your way in
- Provide elbow room
- Use elbow grease
- Sharp elbows
- Rub elbows with
- Didn't lift a finger
- Finger food
- Finger lickin' good
- Finger-pointing
- Give the finger
- Hard to put my finger on it
- Have your finger on the pulse
- An itchy trigger finger
- Lay a finger on someone
- Point the finger at someone
- Put your finger on something
- Slip through your fingers
- Twist him around my little finger

- Wet-finger politicians
- Cross your fingers
- Fingers crossed
- Get your fingers burnt
- Hanging on by your fingernails
- Work your fingers to the bone
- At my fingertips
- Close-fisted
- Shake your fist
- Tight-fisted
- A fistful of money
- Get a grip on yourself
- Lose your grip
- Tighten your grip
- Bust a gut
- Go with your gut

Turn your back on someone

- A gut feeling
- A gut reaction
- Split a gut
- A gutless wonder
- Hate his guts

- Have the guts
- No guts, no glory
- A lot of hand-waving
- By hand
- I can count that on the fingers of one hand
- Dismiss you out of hand
- Extend your hand

Take him in hand

- Force your hand
- Get out of hand
- Give a helping hand
- Give me a hand
- You've got to hand it to him
- The hand is quicker than the eye
- Hand it over
- Hand off something
- The hand that rocks the cradle
- A hand-me-down
- Have a hand in something
- A heavy hand

- A hot hand
- A steady hand
- A good hand to play
- Have it at hand
- Have it on hand
- Have the upper hand
- Have your hand in the till
- Have your hand on the wheel
- Have your hand out
- Heavy-handed
- Hold a weak hand
- Hold the winning hand
- Keep a firm hand
- Know it like the back of your hand
- The left hand doesn't know what the right hand is doing
- Lend a hand
- Need a hand
- No one laid a hand on him
- An old hand at
- On the one hand
- On the other hand
- Overplay your hand
- Your right-hand man
- Show your hand
- Sleight of hand
- Take him in hand
- Talk to the hand
- Tip your hand
- Touched by the hand of god

- Try your hand at something
- Waited on hand and foot
- Work hand-in-hand with
- Come away empty-handed
- A left-handed compliment
- An off-handed remark
- Backhanded compliment
- A glad-hander
- She's a handful
- A handoff
- Handpicked
- All hands on deck
- Can't get your hands on it
- Change hands
- Come with clean hands
- Down on your hands and knees
- Fall into the wrong hands
- Get your hands dirty
- My hands are full
- My hands are tied
- Hands down
- Hands-free
- Hands like feet
- Hands off
- A hands-on approach
- Hands-on experience
- A hands-on guy
- Have good hands
- Be in good hands
- It's in safe hands

- Keep your hands to yourself
- Lay your hands on
- Many hands make light work
- It's out of my hands
- Like putty in my hands
- A show of hands
- Take matters into your own hands
- Turn back the hands of time
- Wash your hands of
- Wrap your hands around
- Wring your hands
- Be handsy
- Come in handy
- Keep it handy
- A handyman
- All heart
- Be still my heart
- To believe it with all of your heart
- It'll break my heart
- Cross my heart
- Cry your heart out
- Eat your heart out
- Follow one's heart
- A fool's heart
- Get to the heart of it
- Harden his heart
- Have a change of heart
- Have a heart
- Have a soft heart

- Have your heart in the right place
- Have your heart in your mouth
- Have your heart set on it
- My heart goes out to you
- My heart is in my throat
- Your heart isn't in it
- A heart of gold
- A heart of stone
- My heart skipped a beat
- My heart was in my mouth
- A heartrending situation
- A heart-stopper
- A heart-to-heart talk
- He's her heartthrob
- In my heart of hearts
- The key to my heart
- Learn it by heart

Tug at your heartstrings

- Lose heart
- A loving heart
- A man after my own heart
- Not for the faint of heart
- Over the heart of the plate
- Pour your heart out
- Put your heart and soul into it

- Serious as a heart attack
- Show a big heart
- A sober heart
- Steal her heart
- Take heart
- Take it to heart
- Tear your heart out
- The way to a man's heart is through his stomach
- Weigh heavily on my heart
- With a heavy heart
- With half a heart
- It's a heartache
- Happen in a heartbeat
- Heartbroken
- Good-hearted
- To be kindhearted
- Lighthearted
- Make a halfhearted effort
- Stouthearted
- Truehearted
- Disheartened
- Heartfelt thanks
- A heartless person
- Win hearts and minds
- Tug at your heartstrings
- Hale and hearty
- Party hearty
- Bare-knuckle fight
- Bare-knuckle politics

- Knuckle down
- A knuckle sandwich
- Knuckle under
- Too near the knuckle
- White-knuckle
- A knucklehead
- A nail-biter
- Contemplate your navel
- Navel-gazing
- Grease his palm
- Have him in the palm of my hands

Carry the weight of the world on your shoulders

- Palm it off
- Itchy palms
- Cut to the quick
- Your reach exceeds your grasp
- Give someone a ribbing
- A fair shake
- Always looking over my shoulder

- Have a chip on your shoulder
- Have a shoulder to cry on
- On the shoulders of giants
- Put your shoulder to the wheel
- Shoulder arms
- Shoulder the blame
- Shoulder the burden
- Shoulder the load
- Stand shoulder to shoulder with
- Straight from the shoulder
- Round shouldered
- Carry the weight of the world on your shoulders
- Big shoulders to lean on
- Rub shoulders with someone
- Stand on the shoulders of
- Have no spine
- It sent chills up my spine
- Show some spine
- Can't stomach him
- Cast-iron stomach
- Doesn't have the stomach for something
- Have a stomach bug
- Make me sick to my stomach
- On an empty stomach
- Settle your stomach
- My stomach is tied up in knots
- It turns my stomach
- Put your thumb on the scale
- A rule of thumb

- Stick out like a sore thumb
- Thumb a ride
- Thumb through
- Thumb your nose at something
- Under his thumb
- All thumbs
- Thumbs down
- Thumbs up
- Twiddle your thumbs
- Cut the umbilical cord
- A slap on the wrist
- An ankle biter
- A well-turned ankle
- Breaking ankles
- Bust your butt
- Butt dial
- Butt in
- Butt of the joke
- Butt out
- Cover your butt
- Get off your butt
- Kick someone's butt
- Kiss ass
- A pain in the butt
- Work your butt off
- Dragging your feet
- Fast on your feet
- Feet first
- Find your feet
- Get back on your feet

- Get your feet wet
- Have feet of clay
- Have the world at your feet
- Two left feet
- Hold your feet to the fire
- Jump in with both feet
- Keep both feet on the ground
- Knock you off your feet
- Land on your feet
- Put up your feet
- Stand on your own two feet
- Swept off your feet
- Think on your feet
- Underfoot
- Change is afoot
- Fleet of foot
- Foot of the bed
- Foot the bill
- Footloose and fancy free
- Get a foot in the door
- Get off on the wrong foot
- Have a heavy foot
- Have a lead foot
- One foot in the grave
- One foot out the door
- On your back foot
- Put one foot in front of the other
- Put your best foot forward
- Put your foot down

- Put your foot in it
- Put your foot in your mouth
- A tenderfoot
- Caught flat-footed
- Surefooted
- Gain a foothold
- Gain a footing
- Lose your footing
- On even footing
- On solid footing
- Be put on the right footing
- Regain your footing
- Leave footprints
- Play footsie with
- Follow in his footsteps
- Bring someone to heel

Lap it up

- Down-at-the-heel
- Be a heel
- Well-heeled
- Back on its heels
- Come on the heels of
- Dig in your heels
- Drag your heels
- Keep on your heels

- Kick up your heels
- Right on your heels
- Have in your hip pocket
- Hip-hop
- Hip, hip, hooray!
- Joined at the hip
- Come on bended knee
- Knee-deep in something
- A knee-jerk reaction
- A knee-slapper
- Take a knee
- Knock-kneed
- Brought to your knees
- Cut him off at the knees
- Weak in the knees
- Fall into your lap
- Lap it up
- It's now in your lap
- Break a leg
- Do the legwork
- Get a leg up
- I'm just pulling your leg
- Shake a leg
- Have legs
- Bring up the rear
- Sit a spell
- Sit on it!
- Sit on your hands
- Sit tight

- I won't sit still for that
- Sitting pretty
- I can't stand it
- He can't stand the pace
- Don't stand on ceremony
- A last stand
- Make a stand
- On the stand
- Stand a chance
- Stand by me
- Stand down
- Stand firm
- Stand in for
- Stand on principle
- Stand pat
- Stand tall
- Stand up for what's right
- Stand up for yourself
- Stand-alone
- A stand-up comic
- Take a stand
- United we stand
- Where we stand
- I won't stand for it
- As it stands
- A false step
- Pep in your step
- Stop chasing your own tail
- Dip your toe in the water
- Tiptoe around it

- Toe the line
- Toe the mark
- Gain a toehold
- Keep you on your toes
- Tickle your toes
- Bad blood between them
- Blood brothers
- There'll be blood in the streets
- Blood in the water
- Blood is thicker than water
- Blood on the carpet
- A blood pact
- Blood runs cold
- Blood-curdling
- Blood, sweat, and tears
- Bring in new blood
- Draw blood
- Get the blood flowing
- Have blood on your hands
- It's in your blood
- Make my blood boil
- A bloodbath
- Bloody hell
- Bloody mess
- Get bodied
- Know where the bodies are buried
- Body language
- Body of water
- The body politic

- Body slam
- A busybody
- An out-of-body experience
- Working the body
- Bad to the bone
- A bone of contention
- Bone up on something
- Bone-rattling
- Boneheaded
- Close to the bone
- Cut to the bone
- Doesn't have a mean bone in his body
- Dry as a bone
- Have a bone to pick with someone
- Left bone-dry
- Skin and bone
- Tickle his funny bone
- With every bone in my body
- Big-boned
- Small-boned
- He's all bones
- Bare-bones budget
- Jump your bones
- Lazybones
- Make no bones about it
- Flesh out
- In the flesh
- My own flesh and blood
- Press the flesh

- The spirit is willing, but the flesh is weak
- Bust up the joint
- Don't move a muscle
- A muscle head
- Muscle memory
- Muscle your way into
- Put some muscle behind it
- Show muscle
- Find the nerve
- Have a lot of nerve
- Lose your nerve
- The nerve of him
- Nerve-wracking
- A raw nerve
- Strike a nerve
- A bundle of nerves
- Get on each other's nerves
- Grate on my nerves
- Nerves of steel
- Rattle nerves
- A show of nerves
- Be quite nervy
- Left with a skeleton staff
- Your family skeletons
- Know where the skeletons are
- Skeletons in the closet
- Beauty is only skin deep
- Comfortable in your own skin
- Escape by the skin of your teeth

- Get under my skin
- Give me some skin
- Have no skin in the game
- Jump out of your skin
- It makes my skin crawl
- No skin off my back
- No skin off my nose
- Save your own skin
- Show some skin
- Skin him alive
- Be thick skinned
- Thin-skinned
- Course through your veins

Skeletons in the closet

BUILDING & CONSTRUCTION

1.

2.

3.

1. Cut it out! 2. On a pedestal 3. A hole in the wall

A blockhead

- Back on the beam
- Beaming with pride
- Knock your block off
- A stumbling block
- A blockhead
- Across the board
- Go by the board
- Stiff as a board
- Brace yourself
- Bric-a-brac
- A brick-and-mortar operation
- Dumb as a brick
- Hit a brick wall
- Just another brick in the wall
- One brick short of a load
- Thick as a brick
- A few bricks shy of a load

- It hit me like a ton of bricks
- Hit the bricks
- A bridge to the past
- Build it from scratch
- A new build
- The building blocks of life
- Building up a head of steam
- Built from the ground up
- Built on sand
- A cardboard cutout
- Concrete jungle
- Set in concrete
- Slip through the cracks
- A cut above
- A cut above the rest
- Cut and dried
- Cut and paste
- Cut and run
- Cut him some slack
- Cut it out!
- Cut to pieces
- Make the cut
- It cuts both ways
- On the cutting edge

Just another brick in the wall

- A danger zone
- All decked out
- An elevator pitch
- Don't fence me in
- A fence-sitter
- On the fence
- Play both sides of the fence
- Mend fences
- The fix is in
- If it ain't broke, don't fix it

Don't fence me in

- In a fix
- No easy fix
- A quick fix
- A fixer-upper
- Floor it
- A floor model
- Get in on the ground floor
- Given the floor
- Pick yourself up off the floor
- Take the floor
- Be floored
- Lay the foundation
- Come unhinged

- They don't make 'em like that anymore
- Make do
- Make something out of nothing
- Break the mold
- Cast in the same mold
- Knocked off your pedestal
- On a pedestal
- Knocked down a peg or two
- From pillar to post
- A pillar of strength
- A pillar of the community
- A lead-pipe cinch
- Pipe down
- It went down the wrong pipe
- In the pipeline
- Between the pipes
- Walk the plank
- Packed to the rafters
- Shake to the rafters
- Make things right
- Put it right
- Right away
- Hold the room together
- Hang out your shingle
- Steamroll it through
- Tar beach
- Tarred with the same brush
- A teardown
- Build a big tent

- Fold up your tent
- Go to the wall for
- The great wall
- A hole in the wall
- Off the wall
- Up against the wall
- Walled off
- Building walls between us

- If these walls could talk
- The walls have ears
- It's just window dressing
- It's out the window
- A window of opportunity
- Come out of the woodwork
- Like a wrecking ball

Walk the plank

BUSINESS & WORK

1.

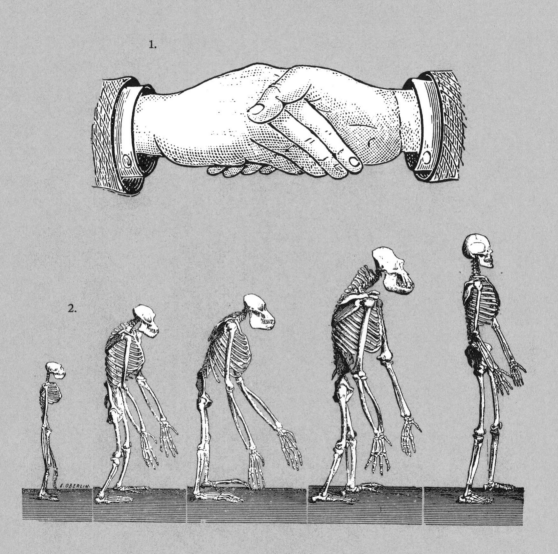

2.

- False advertising
- A hidden agenda
- What's on the agenda?
- Bankers' hours
- Drive a hard bargain
- Keep up your end of the bargain
- More than you bargained for
- Fill the bill
- Fit the bill
- It's a boondoggle
- Borrow to the hilt
- You're the boss
- All business
- Back in business
- Back to business
- Big business
- Business as usual
- Business before pleasure
- Business first
- The first order of business
- Get down to business
- I mean business
- Mind your own business
- No funny business
- Like nobody's business
- Slippery business
- Taking care of business
- Unfinished business
- Buy and sell you
- Buy in to something

- Buy low, sell high
- I don't buy it
- Let the buyer beware
- Buyer's remorse
- Cross-check
- Out of commission
- A company man
- In mixed company
- In select company
- Have connections
- Make connections
- A consumer trap
- Corporate culture
- Behind the counter
- Under the counter
- Give credit where credit is due
- Take the credit
- The customer is always right
- Know your customer
- A regular customer
- A tough customer
- What's the damage?
- Ace the deal
- Back out of the deal
- A big deal
- Clinch the deal
- Cut a deal
- Deal with it
- A done deal
- Get a raw deal

- It's a helluva deal
- Make a deal behind closed doors
- A package deal
- What's the big deal?
- What's the deal?
- A dealmaker
- It will take some doing
- Get it done
- Earn your keep
- Trickle-down economics
- Voodoo economics
- Free enterprise
- You're fired!
- The gig economy
- A side gig
- He's damaged goods
- Deliver the goods
- Get the goods
- A handshake is my word
- Last hired, first fired
- A side hustle
- Titans of industry
- A bang-up job
- A botch job
- Don't give up your day job
- Fall down on the job
- It gets the job done
- A good job
- Have what it takes to do the job

In the market for

- An inside job
- Job security
- Land a job
- Lie down on the job
- Like it's your J.O.B.
- On the job
- On-the-job training
- Put your job on the line
- A rush job
- Take this job and shove it
- Between jobs
- A joint effort
- Keep at it
- Belabor the point
- A labor of love
- Labor over something
- A new lease on life
- A loss-leader
- The bottom fell out of the market
- Deal in the black market
- In the market for

- On the market
- Priced out of the market
- Micromanage
- Cut out the middleman
- Get something for nothing
- A limited-time offer
- An offer you can't refuse
- I gave at the office
- Own it
- That's above my pay grade
- An honest day's pay
- On the payroll
- Cross the picket line
- It all went according to plan
- Quick and dirty
- High turnover rate
- Acknowledge receipt
- Show me the receipts
- Tender your resignation
- A clearance sale
- An estate sale
- A tag sale
- A sales pitch
- Ahead of schedule
- Behind schedule
- Don't sell him short
- A hard sell
- Sell at a loss
- Sell for parts
- Sell someone out

- He'd sell his mother
- Seller's remorse
- At your service
- Close shop
- One-stop shop
- Open up shop
- Set up shop
- Sign off
- Sign on the dotted line
- Soft skills
- Sold a bill of goods
- Be sold on it
- Do me a solid
- Split the difference
- Your stock in trade
- Taking stock
- Give away the store
- A mom-and-pop store
- Who's minding the store?
- For the taking

Sign on the dotted line

- A to-do list
- A trade-off

Hard at work

- Tricks of the trade
- Follow the paper trail
- Follow the trail
- Leave a paper trail
- Put to good use
- Make yourself useful
- A wage gap
- A wage hike
- Get it wholesale
- All in a day's work
- Do the dirty work
- Get down to work
- Hard at work
- Have your work cut out for you
- An honest day's work
- Keep up the good work
- Make fast work of it

- Make short work of it
- Nice work if you can get it
- Part-time work
- He's a piece of work
- Put them to work
- Strong work
- Work around the clock
- Work from the bottom up
- My work here is done
- A work in progress
- Work in tandem
- Work it out
- Work like a dog
- Work like the devil
- Work like the dickens
- Work off the books
- Work out the kinks

- Work overtime
- Work until you drop
- Work your tail off
- Work your way up
- Work yourself to death
- All worked up
- In working order
- Working at cross-purposes
- A working girl
- A working stiff
- In the works
- Whatever works for you
- Works for me
- It works like a charm

COLORS

1.

2.

1. White as a ghost   2. A white elephant

A black sheep

- Black as a skillet
- The Black Death
- A black eye
- Black Friday
- A black hole
- Black humor
- Black magic
- A black mark on your record
- Black money
- Black out
- A black sheep
- A black swan
- Black-tie
- In the black
- Jet black
- Little black book
- The new black
- Pitch-black
- Black and blue
- It's not black and white
- Blackball

- Blacken your name
- Blacklist
- Blackmail
- Blue blood
- Blue chip
- A blue-collar worker
- Blue-dog democrats
- Blue laws
- Blue Monday
- A blue-plate special
- Blue ribbon
- Blue-penciled
- A bluestocking
- A bolt from the blue
- Feeling blue
- Out of the clear blue sky
- Talk a blue streak
- True blue
- Wild blue yonder

- Brown bagging
- Brownnose
- A brownout
- You're giving me gray hair
- A gray area
- Gray divorce
- The old gray lady
- Shades of gray
- Given the green light
- Go green
- Be green
- Green around the gills
- Green as a gooseberry
- Green as grass
- A green-collar worker
- Green politics
- A green room
- A green thumb
- Green with envy

Green with envy

- Raking in the green
- Be too green
- A needle in a haystack
- A pink slip
- In the pink
- Tickled pink
- Paint a rosy picture
- Rosy-cheeked
- Born to the purple
- Purple heart
- Purple prose
- Bleed red ink
- Caught red-handed
- Crossing the red line
- Cut through the red tape
- Draw a red line
- Give the red light
- In the red
- Not one red cent
- Paint the town red
- Raise a red flag
- A red alert
- Red as a beet
- The red-carpet treatment
- A red herring
- Red hot
- The red scare
- The red zone
- The red-eye
- A red-letter day

- Red-tag something
- See red
- Wave a red rag to a bull
- Bleed red, white, and blue
- Raise the white flag
- Ride in on a white horse
- White as a ghost
- White as the driven snow
- White coat syndrome
- White-collar crime
- A white-collar worker
- A white elephant
- The white-glove treatment
- White heat
- A white knight
- A white lie
- White noise
- Like white on rice
- A white paper
- A white sale
- Whiteout conditions
- Whitewash
- An amber alert
- An amber gambler
- Follow the yellow-brick road
- A yellow-dog contract
- A yellow-dog democrat
- Yellow journalism
- Yellow streak
- Yellow-bellied

Caught red-handed

- Have a clear conscience
- Be in the clear
- Break the color line
- Change your color
- Color inside the lines
- Color outside the lines
- Color your thinking
- In glorious Technicolor
- In living color
- Lend color to it
- Local color
- Off-color
- These colors don't run
- Pass with flying colors
- Show your true colors
- Stay true to your colors
- Pale in comparison

COMING & GOING

Come on in, the water's fine

- The best is yet to come
- You've come a long way, baby
- Come across well
- Come alive
- Come around to
- It'll come as no surprise
- Come at
- Come back from the brink
- Come back into the fold
- Come back to bite you
- Come back to haunt you
- Come back with a vengeance
- Come before
- Come close
- Come crawling back
- Come down on
- Come down the pike
- Come down with
- Come forward
- Come from the bottom
- A come-hither look
- Come into line
- Come off it
- Come on in, the water's fine
- Come out of the blue
- Come out on top
- Come over
- To come running
- Come through something
- Come to a boil

You've come a long way, baby

- Come to a standstill
- Come to an impasse
- Come to fruition
- Come to grief
- Come to grips with it
- Come to life
- Come to no avail
- Come to nothing
- Come to pass
- Come to regret
- Come to the forefront
- Come to the rescue
- Come to the surface
- Come together
- Come under
- Come up dry
- Come up for air
- Come up smiling
- Come upon
- Come what may
- Come with the territory
- The comedown
- Oh, come now

- Whatever may come
- Here comes trouble
- What goes around comes around
- Like Christmas coming early
- A coming attraction
- Coming in hot
- Coming on like gangbusters
- Coming on strong
- Coming on the scene
- You've got another thing coming
- I saw that coming from a mile away
- Up and coming
- Can't tell if he's coming or going
- It comes and goes

Come to a boil

- Easy come, easy go
- Have you coming and going
- From the get-go
- Get it to go
- Give the go-ahead
- Go ahead
- Go all out
- Go along for the ride
- Go along with
- Go ape over
- Go astray
- To go at
- Go awry
- Go ballistic
- Go behind his back
- Go belly-up
- Go beyond
- Go bonkers
- Go commando
- Go for the jugular
- Go get 'em, tiger
- To go hand in hand
- Go head-to-head
- Go in with your eyes wide open
- Go into detail
- Go jump in the lake
- Go live
- Go off
- Go off the reservation
- Go out on a high note

- Go out on top
- Go out with a bang
- Go over
- Go public
- Go right to the heart of the matter
- Go rogue
- Things go south
- Go the extra mile
- Go through a good spell
- Go through a rough patch
- Go through the motions
- Go through with
- Go to extremes
- Go to pieces
- Go to seed
- Go to wrack and ruin
- Go toe-to-toe
- Go with the territory
- Go wrong
- Go your merry way
- Good to go
- Have a go at it
- A no-go
- Raring to go
- Steady as we go
- Time to go
- There goes the neighborhood
- That's the way it goes
- Everything going for her

Go jump in the lake

- Going downhill
- Going my way?
- Going places
- The going rate
- Going south
- Going the right way
- Going to town
- Going, going, gone
- Have a good thing going
- Keep going
- Keep it going
- I must be going
- There's no going back
- Really get going
- Slow going
- A foregone conclusion
- As good as gone
- Let bygones be bygones

COMMUNICATION

1.

2.

- Advise against
- Take it under advisement
- Agree to disagree
- I couldn't agree more
- Don't take "no" for an answer
- A soft answer turneth away wrath
- For the sake of argument
- It depends on who you ask
- Asked and answered
- You're asking for it
- You're asking for trouble
- Set up a backchannel
- My bad
- I beg to differ
- Beg your pardon
- Blah, blah, blah
- Don't bother
- No bother
- Quit bothering me
- Bragging rights
- Break the news
- I hate to break it to you
- Let me break it down for you
- Answer the call
- It's anyone's call
- At your beck and call
- Call dibs
- A call for change
- Call him out

- Call in your chits
- I call it like I see it
- Call it off
- Call it quits
- Call it right
- The call of the wild
- Call off the dogs
- Call out
- A catcall
- A clarion call
- A crank call
- Don't call us, we'll call you
- A gutsy call
- Last call
- On call
- Pay a call
- A prank call
- Too close to call
- It's a tough call
- It's a wake-up call
- It's your call
- Called to account
- Called upon
- Be your calling card
- Find your calling
- It's a higher calling
- I can't complain
- I can't even
- Charmed, I'm sure

- Let me make myself perfectly clear
- Loud and clear
- A sidebar conversation
- Strike up a conversation
- Copy that
- The crux of the matter
- Damage control
- That's debatable
- There's no denying it
- All over the dial
- Dial it back
- Dial it down
- Don't touch that dial
- I have you on speed dial
- Up for discussion
- Ditto
- No doubt
- No doubt about it
- Drivel on
- If I had my druthers
- Easy does it
- A lame excuse
- That's no excuse
- I'm all out of excuses
- Fine with me
- Be flabbergasted
- Flattery will get you nowhere
- Quite frankly
- Pardon my French

- Make fun of someone
- Poke fun at
- The gift of gab
- I get it
- Get the giggles
- Gobbledygook
- It's all good
- Goodbye for now
- Gossip monger
- Your guess is as good as mine
- It just so happens
- Have it your way
- Take a hint
- Honest to goodness
- Howdy, partner
- As if
- It's iffy
- No ifs, ands, or buts
- For all intents and purposes
- Crack a joke
- An inside joke
- The joke is on you
- It's no joke
- A standing joke
- Take a joke
- Keep it to yourself
- Keep quiet about
- Keep to yourself
- As far as I know
- I don't know what to make of it

- In plain language
- Watch your language
- Leave it be
- A dirty lie
- What lies ahead

Smooth operator

- Take liberties
- Till we meet again
- We have to stop meeting like this
- I didn't get the memo
- Don't mention it
- Mention in passing
- Don't mess with me
- Get the message
- Mixed message
- Be off-message
- It sends the wrong message
- Stay on-message
- Blame the messenger
- Render him mute
- Mutter under your breath
- The bearer of bad news
- Breaking news

- No news is good news
- Make nice
- Get the nod
- Make noise about something
- Duly noted
- Advance notice
- No offense
- Smooth operator
- In my humble opinion
- A matter of opinion
- Not a peep outta you
- Be peeved
- Call the batphone
- Hold the phone
- Just a phone call away
- Phone it in
- The phones are ringing off the hook
- Keep it plain and simple
- Always a pleasure
- Get to the punch line
- I have no qualms about it
- Raise a fuss
- Raise a hue and cry
- Rant and rave
- Reach out
- Be real
- For real?
- Get real
- Need I remind you

- With all due respect
- In some respects
- Respond in kind
- Give a wishy-washy response
- A clever retort
- Right back at you
- Right you are
- Have a familiar ring
- Ring my bell
- Ring you up
- Rumor has it
- Better left unsaid
- Easier said than done
- To echo what was said
- He said, she said
- Said no one, ever
- There's something to be said for
- When all is said and done
- As they say
- Do as I say
- Have a say in
- Have the final say
- It's not what you say, it's how you say it
- Need I say more?
- Needless to say
- Never say never
- It's not for me to say
- Say a few words
- Say it ain't so

- Say my piece
- To say the least
- Sorry to say
- I hate to be a naysayer
- It goes without saying
- It says a lot about you
- That says it all
- The inside scoop
- She's a scream
- A dirty little secret
- Shout from the rooftops
- A shouting match
- Shut your trap
- Send the wrong signal
- Send out mixed signals
- Smoke signals
- Smooth over
- Is that so?
- Get through to someone
- Get something across
- Something or other
- Something tells me
- That was something else
- Have a spat
- He doesn't speak our language
- So to speak
- Speak for yourself
- Speak ill
- Speak in broken English
- Speak in tongues

- Speak now or forever hold your peace
- Speak off-the-cuff
- Speak only when spoken to
- Speak the same language
- Speak too soon
- Speak truth to power
- Speak with a silver tongue
- Speak your mind
- Speak your piece
- Speaking of which . . .
- Think before you speak
- In a manner of speaking
- Loosely speaking
- Roughly speaking
- He speaks our lingo
- It speaks volumes
- Spoken for
- Give a spiel
- Make a statement
- Kept in suspense
- What do you take me for?
- All talk and no action
- Cross talk
- Girl talk
- Guy talk
- Plain talk
- Real talk
- Smooth talker
- Straight talk

- Sweet-talk someone
- Talk a good game
- Talk a good line
- Talk back
- Talk behind someone's back
- Talk down to
- Talk is cheap
- Talk it up
- Talk of the town
- Talk out of school
- Talk sense into
- Talk shop
- Talk someone into something
- Talk someone's ear off
- Talk the hind legs off a donkey
- Talk through your hat
- Talk tough
- Talk until you're blue in the face
- Talk you through it
- Tough talk
- Close talker
- Now you're talkin'
- Look who's talking
- Talking heads
- Like talking to a brick wall
- Trash talking
- Taken to task
- A tattle tale
- Do tell
- If I tell you, I'll have to kill you

- Never tell tales out of school
- To not be able to tell
- Show and tell
- Show, don't tell
- Tell all
- Tell it like it is
- Tell it to the marines
- A telltale sign
- You tell me
- Is that a thing?
- Who do you think you are?
- Hold that thought
- Hold true
- Too true
- True to type
- Ain't that the truth?
- Many a truth is said in jest
- Truth be told
- Try as you might

- Have a voice in something
- Make your voice heard
- An indoor voice
- An outdoor voice
- Wail like a banshee
- No matter what
- So what?
- To what end?
- What seems to be the problem here?
- What's not to like?
- What's the scoop?
- Whisper down the lane
- Why bother?
- Why I oughta
- Be careful what you wish for
- Don't get me wrong
- Yada, yada, yada

True to type

CONTAINERS

Have you over a barrel

- Bag and baggage
- Bag it
- A bag of bones
- A bag of tricks
- He couldn't find his way out of a paper bag
- A dirtbag
- It's in the bag
- Left holding the bag
- A mixed bag
- Not my bag
- A swag bag
- Have bags under your eyes
- Barrel into someone
- As crooked as a barrel of fishhooks
- Have you over a barrel
- More fun than a barrel of monkeys
- He's no barrel of laughs
- Scrape the bottom of the barrel
- Cash on the barrelhead
- A basket case
- In the same basket
- Bottle up your emotions
- A bottleneck
- The genie is out of the bottle
- Boxed in
- A chatterbox
- Check the box
- On a soapbox

- Think outside the box
- A tinderbox
- The bucket list
- Coming down in buckets
- It doesn't amount to a bucket of spit
- Kick the bucket
- A slime bucket
- A can of worms
- An empty vessel makes the most noise
- In the can

- Kick the can down the road
- Canned laughter
- Get canned
- Argue the other side of the case
- Back on the case
- Case closed
- Case in point
- Case law
- A case of the blues
- A case of the Mondays

Scrape the bottom of the barrel

Stir the pot

- A case study
- A cold case
- Don't make a federal case of it
- Duck a case
- You got a good case
- A head case
- Make a case for
- On someone's case
- On the case
- An open-and-shut case
- Plead your case
- I rest my case
- Take up your case
- A textbook case
- A best-case scenario
- A worst-case scenario

- Collect yourself
- Cover for someone
- A cover-up
- Dish out dirt
- Flip your lid
- Keep a lid on it
- There's a lid for every pot
- A fusspot
- Gone to pot
- Handy as a small pot
- Keep the pot boiling
- A melting pot
- Stir the pot
- Sweeten the pot
- A watched pot never boils
- Get the sack
- Hit the sack
- A sad sack
- Get sacked
- Have something left in the tank
- A think tank
- Down the tubes
- Fill a void

EARTH, FIRE, WATER & AIR

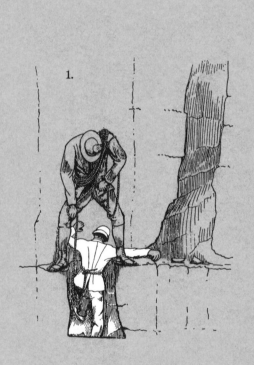

1. Dig yourself out of a hole   2. Dig for dirt   3. Stoke the fires

- A beach bum
- A beached whale
- Push the boundaries
- Go over the cliff
- A cliff-hanger
- The coast is clear
- Dig deep
- Dig for dirt
- Dig in
- Dig to China
- Dig up
- Dig up the skeletons
- I dig you
- Dig your grave with your own knife and fork
- Dig your way out
- Dig yourself into a hole
- Dig yourself out of a hole
- Take a dig at someone
- Dug in
- Common as dirt

A cliff-hanger

- Dirt cheap
- Dirt-poor
- Get the dirt on someone
- Grovel in the dirt
- Sling dirt
- Treated like dirt
- Down and dirty
- Talk dirty
- A last-ditch effort
- In the boondocks
- Bite the dust
- Collect dust
- Dry as dust
- Left in the dust
- Wait until the dust settles
- The ol' dusty trail
- Blanket the earth with
- Brought down to earth
- Come down to earth
- Disappear from the face of the earth
- Down-to-earth
- An earth mother
- Earth-shattering
- How on earth could that happen?
- A scorched-earth tactic
- The scum of the earth
- What on earth is going on?
- Willing to go to the ends of the earth

Find common ground

- Earthly desires
- Be earthy
- The fault line
- Generous to a fault
- Flood the zone
- Break new ground
- A breeding ground
- Cover a lot of ground
- Cut the ground out from under you
- Fertile ground
- Find common ground
- Gain ground
- Give ground
- Hit the ground running
- Hold your ground
- Losing ground
- Make up lost ground
- It never got off the ground
- On good ground
- On solid ground
- Stand on shaky ground

- Stand your ground
- Take the high ground
- Take the middle ground
- Grounded
- Grounded in the fundamentals
- Your fears are groundless
- The old stomping grounds
- On what grounds?
- A groundswell
- Lay the groundwork for
- Go downhill
- Over hill and dale
- Over the hill
- A tough hill to climb
- Up the hill
- Head for the hills
- Fall into a deep hole
- Holed up
- Poke holes in
- Take it to the hole
- La-La Land
- Land it
- The land of nod
- Land of opportunity
- Land of plenty
- The lay of the land
- Never-Never Land
- No-man's-land
- Stuck in the mire
- Wallow in the mire

- Climb the highest mountain
- Move mountains
- Reach over the mountaintop
- Common as muck
- Muckety-mucks
- Muck it up
- Clear as mud
- Dragged through the mud
- Have mud on your face
- Here's mud in your eye
- Sling mud
- Reach the peak
- In a rut
- Bring sand to the beach
- Pound sand
- Uncharted territory
- Protect your turf
- Turf it off
- A turf war
- The uncanny valley
- All corners of the world
- All's right with the world
- Bring into the world
- Depart from this world
- Without a care in the world
- First-world problems
- Have the world by the tail
- In another world
- In one's own world
- The leader of the free world

- You mean the world to me
- Move up in the world
- It's not the end of the world
- You only go through this world once
- Otherworldly
- Out of this world
- Out to change the world
- Sitting on top of the world
- Think the world of someone
- Turn his world upside down
- Turn the world on its ears
- That's what makes the world go 'round
- The world is passing you by
- The world is your oyster
- A world of difference
- A world of good
- A world of hurt
- World-class
- I wouldn't miss it for the world
- Be worldly
- Worlds apart
- Useful as an ashtray on a motorbike
- Rise from the ashes
- Go out in a blaze of glory
- Go to blazes
- Burn notice
- Burn some clock
- Burn someone

- Burn the candle at both ends
- Burn the midnight oil
- Crash and burn
- Get burned
- A slow burn
- Burned out
- Burned to a crisp
- Put it on the back burner
- Put it on the front burner
- A burning issue
- A burning question
- He can't hold a candle to someone
- Not fit to hold a candle
- Not worth the candle
- Carry coals
- Rake over the coals
- Add fuel to the fire
- Come under fire
- Create a firestorm
- A dumpster fire
- A fiery debate
- Fight fire with fire
- Fire and brimstone
- Fire in the hole
- A fire sale
- Fire up
- A firebrand
- Go through fire and water
- Light a fire under him

- Light my fire
- On fire
- Play with fire, and you'll get burned
- Play with fire
- Pour gasoline on the fire
- Set the world on fire
- Spread like wildfire
- A surefire way
- Where's the fire?
- Fired up
- Stoke the fires
- A fireside chat
- A flaming liberal
- An old flame
- Fan the flames
- Go down in flames
- Flaming hot
- In a flash
- All smoke and mirrors
- End in smoke
- Put that in your pipe and smoke it
- Smoke like a chimney
- Smoke signals
- A smokescreen
- Up in smoke
- When the smoke clears
- Where there's smoke, there's fire
- Not a spark of decency
- Carry a torch

Carry a torch

- Pass the torch
- Take a bath on
- Hold at bay
- Gone around the bend
- Boil something down
- Boil the ocean
- Bubble over with enthusiasm
- Burst someone's bubble
- On the bubble
- Up the creek without a paddle
- Drown your sorrows
- Like a drowned rat
- Drowning in money
- Drowning in paperwork
- Dry up
- Open the floodgates
- Ebb and flow
- Go with the flow
- Break the ice
- It cuts no ice with me
- Iced-out
- Put on ice

- The tip of the iceberg
- An icebreaker
- Deep as the ocean
- A drop in the ocean
- Oceans apart
- A spit in the ocean
- Take the plunge
- Across the pond
- A ripple effect
- A ripple of excitement
- Cry me a river
- Follow the sea
- A sea change
- On a slippery slope
- Soaked to the bone
- A damp squib
- Do it under your own steam
- Gather steam
- Lose steam
- Pick up steam
- Run out of steam
- Take the steam out of it
- In dire straits
- Cross the stream where it's shallowest
- Drain the swamp
- Swamped with work
- A rising tide lifts all boats
- Roll with the tide
- Stem the tide

- The tide has come in
- The tide wouldn't take him out
- Tide you over
- Turn the tide
- Surf and turf
- Get the vapors
- A washout
- Above water
- It doesn't hold water
- Feeling underwater
- The high-water mark
- The low-water mark
- Something in the water
- Tread water
- Underwater
- Water it down
- Water over the dam
- Water under the bridge
- Watered down
- Watering hole
- Calm the waters
- In calmer waters
- Heading into dangerous waters
- Muddy the waters
- Murky waters
- Still waters run deep
- Stir the waters
- In troubled waters
- In uncharted waters
- Untested waters

- A watershed moment
- The new wave
- Come in waves
- Make waves
- Back to the well
- The well has run dry
- All wet
- An air of pretension
- An air of superiority
- Air one's grievances
- Appear out of thin air
- A breath of fresh air
- Clear the air
- Let the air out of
- Put on airs
- Something in the air
- Suck the air out of the room
- Up in the air
- Vanish into thin air
- Walking on air
- An airhead
- Before you can draw a breath
- Catch the wind in your sails
- Long-winded
- Take the wind out of his sails

EDUCATION

Do the math

- An add-on
- It doesn't add up
- An answer to all your problems
- No easy answers
- Be on your best behavior
- Book smart
- Crack the books
- Hit the books
- A back-of-the-envelope calculation
- Like chalk and cheese
- Chalk it up to experience
- Cheat sheet
- Cheats never prosper
- A class act
- The class clown
- The class cutup
- Cut class
- In a class by itself
- Give it the old college try
- Not college material
- I stand corrected
- Not the brightest crayon in the box
- Crib notes
- Pique your curiosity
- Dumb as a doornail
- Dumbed-down
- Struck dumb
- Easy as ABC
- An educated guess

- "A" for effort
- All things being equal
- After the fact
- A fun fact
- In point of fact
- A little-known fact
- As a matter of fact
- Alternative facts
- Get your facts straight
- I figured as much

No easy answers

- Geek out
- A stroke of genius
- Failing grade
- Make the grade
- Hazard a guess
- Ancient history
- Do your homework
- Feigned ignorance
- Ignorance is bliss
- Before you know it

- In the know
- Know a thing or two
- Know what you are about
- A know-it-all
- More than you know
- A little knowledge is a dangerous thing
- Drop knowledge
- Knowledge is power
- Pool of knowledge
- Learn about it firsthand
- Learn it at your mother's knee
- You learn something new every day
- Learn the hard way
- Learn the ropes
- The learning curve
- Close to the mark
- Leave your mark
- Make your mark
- Mark up
- Miss the mark
- Off the mark
- On your mark . . .
- Right on the mark
- Slow off the mark
- Wide of the mark
- Do the math
- Commit to memory
- An honest mistake
- Make no mistake about it

- Nerd alert
- Nerd out
- Pencil me in
- Realize your potential
- What's your problem?
- An absentminded professor
- Get with the program
- An age-old question
- Beg the question
- Call into question
- No question about it
- There's no such thing as a stupid question
- An open question
- A trick question
- Field questions
- No questions asked
- A pop quiz
- Tarnish your record
- The exception that proves the rule
- Back-to-school sale
- The new school
- The school of hard knocks
- A school of thought
- Too cool for school
- Get schooled
- A run-on sentence
- Earn a sheepskin
- He is a blank slate
- Wipe the slate clean

- Smart as a whip
- Too smart for your own good
- Fall under your spell
- Spell it out
- Squeak through
- A quick study
- Needed to be taught a lesson
- A teachable moment
- Experience is the best teacher
- The teacher's pet
- Test the waters
- Test your mettle
- Give it a think
- Think ahead
- Think fast
- Think long and hard about it
- Think nothing of it

- Do the unthinkable
- Forward-thinking
- The power of positive thinking
- Wishful thinking
- Just a thought
- That's the conventional wisdom
- A nugget of wisdom
- Wise beyond his years
- None the wiser
- At wit's end
- Gather your wits
- Keep your wits about you
- Scare the wits out of him

Too cool for school

EXCLAMATIONS

Oh, rats!

Drop dead!

- At that!
- Awesome!
- Bingo!
- Bupkis!
- Come on over!
- Drop dead!
- Egads!
- Eureka!
- Gee-whiz!
- Get lost!
- Get out of here!
- Get out of town!
- Get over it!
- Give him the old heave-ho!
- Give me a break!
- Golly!
- Good grief!
- Good luck!
- Got it!
- Gotcha!

- Hang in there!
- Holy smokes!
- Hot diggity dog!
- Hot dog!
- How about that!
- How dare you!
- Hubba-hubba!
- Hurrah!
- Hurry up!
- Lights out!
- Nah!
- No problem!
- Oh dear!
- Oh my!
- Oh no!
- Oh yeah!
- Oh, fiddlesticks!
- Oh, rats!
- Onward and upward!
- Oops!
- Ouch!
- Oy vey!
- Phooey!
- Really!
- Ship ahoy!
- That's all, folks!
- That's life!
- Trust me!
- Ugh!
- Way to go!

- What a pity!
- When you got it, you got it!
- Whoopee!
- Wicked awesome!
- Woe is me!
- Wow!
- Yahoo!
- Yikes!
- Yippee!
- You bet!
- You don't say!
- You go, girl!
- You wish!
- You're on!
- You're telling me!
- You've got to be kidding me!
- Yuck!

Holy smokes!

EXERCISE

1. Like riding a bicycle 2. Off and running

- Lower the bar
- Raise the bar
- Reset the bar
- Set the bar high
- Feel the burn
- He acts like a dumbbell
- An exercise in futility
- Feel fit

- Survival of the fittest
- Flex your muscles
- Weird flex, but okay
- A gym rat
- Mental gymnastics
- Give someone a lift
- Do the heavy lifting
- Locker room talk

- Might makes right
- With all your might
- Pump iron
- Like riding a bicycle
- Get ripped
- Ripped from the headlines
- Ripped to shreds
- An end-run
- You gave it a good run
- We had a good run
- Make a run for it
- On the run
- Run a country mile
- Run a red light
- Run amok
- Run circles around you
- Run for cover
- Run for the hills
- A run for the roses
- Run for your life
- Run into headwinds
- Run into roadblocks
- Run into someone
- Run it back
- Run it by someone
- Run it into the ground
- Run it up the flagpole
- Run late
- Run like hell
- Run like the devil

Flex your muscles

- Run like the dickens
- Run like the wind
- Run out of town
- Run out the clock
- Run rings around someone
- Run roughshod over
- Run the gamut
- Run the gauntlet
- Run the show
- Run the table
- Run time
- Run with it
- Run your mouth off
- Run yourself ragged
- A run-up
- You can run but you can't hide
- Get the runaround
- Give me the rundown
- A front-runner
- In the running
- Off and running
- Running for the doors
- A running start
- Running to stand still
- Running water
- Running with the herd
- Up and running
- It runs deep
- It runs in the family
- Skip a beat

- He's no slouch
- In the final stretch
- Stretch the truth
- That's a stretch
- Stretched to the limit
- Still going strong
- Break out in a sweat
- By the sweat of my brow
- Don't sweat the small stuff
- A flop sweat
- No sweat!
- Sweat blood
- Sweat bullets
- Sweat equity
- Sweat it out
- Sweat like a pig
- Sweat like a sinner in church
- Sweat like a snowman in hell
- A sweatshop
- Without breaking a sweat
- Work up a sweat
- Get swole
- It's a treadmill
- Pull your weight

That's a stretch

FARM

Like a shepherd leads his flock

Crop up

- A barn burner
- Burn down the barn
- He can't hit the broad side of a barn
- A country bumpkin
- A bumper crop
- The cream of the crop
- Crop up
- The pick of the crop
- Come a cropper
- Bet the farm
- A bushel and a peck
- Buy the farm
- Down on the farm
- Farm out
- Give away the farm
- Like a shepherd leads his flock
- Cultivate your own garden
- Garden variety
- Led down the garden path
- A grazer
- A harvest moon
- Harvest time
- The hay is in the barn

- Hit the hay
- Make hay while the sun shines
- A haymaker
- A needle in a haystack
- Thrown into the hopper
- Put through the mill
- More grist for the mill
- Run-of-the-mill
- Put out to pasture
- Seek greener pastures
- Plow ahead
- Plow through
- Put your hand to the plow
- Meanwhile, back at the ranch
- Reap the benefits
- Return to your roots
- Root it out
- The root of the matter

- Take root
- Head for the last roundup
- A tough row to hoe
- A bad seed
- Plant a seed in someone's head
- Sow discord
- Sow your wild oats
- Sprout wings
- Come from good stock
- The last straw
- A straw man
- A straw poll
- Grasp at straws
- Go to the well once too often
- Separate the wheat from the chaff
- Taken out to the woodshed

A grazer

FASHION

- Accessory to the crime
- Belt-and-suspenders approach
- Belt it out of the park
- Belt the grape
- The Bible Belt
- The Borscht Belt
- Hit below the belt
- Keep it under your belt
- Tighten your belt
- Put another notch on your belt
- The Rust Belt
- Years under my belt
- Inside the beltway
- Outside the beltway
- Boot camp
- Boot up
- Get the boot
- Put the boot in
- Booted out
- You bet your boots
- Hang up your boots
- Boots on the ground
- Quaking in your boots
- Shaking in his boots
- Tough as old boots
- Pull yourself up by your bootstraps
- Too big for your britches
- Buckle down
- Buckle under

- Buckle up
- Bustle about
- Bright as a button
- A button nose
- Button up
- Cute as a button
- Press the right button
- Push the panic button
- Right on the button
- Buttonhole someone
- Push my buttons
- Put on your thinking cap
- Wear the cap and bells
- A cloak-and-dagger operation
- Cut from the same cloth
- Out of whole cloth
- A man of the cloth
- Clothes make the man
- She's a clotheshorse
- Coat of paint
- Ride his coattails
- Off the cuff
- I can dress you up, but I can't take you out
- Cross-dress
- Dress down
- Dress for success
- A dress rehearsal
- Dress someone down
- Dress up

- All dressed up with no place to go
- Dressed to a tee
- Dress to impress
- Dressed to kill
- Dressed to the hilt
- Dressed to the nines
- A sharp dresser
- A snappy dresser
- A snazzy dresser
- Get dressed down
- Put on your earmuffs
- Out of fashion
- Fashionably late
- Good old-fashioned fun
- Be old-fashioned
- Have a fit
- Close-fitting
- A fringe benefit
- On the fringe of society
- The lunatic fringe
- He didn't lay a glove on me
- Fits like a glove
- Hand in glove
- An iron fist in a velvet glove
- The gloves are off
- Handle with kid gloves
- Come across with the goods
- Don't hang your hat where you can't reach it
- Don't hang all your hats on one hook

- Get the hang of it
- Hang behind
- Hang loose
- It's nothing to hang your hat on
- It's time to hang up your hat
- Hang a left
- Hang a right
- Don't leave me hanging
- Kept hanging
- Hung up
- All hat and no cattle
- All hat and no cowboy
- Hat in hand

Pull off a hat trick

- Here's your hat. What's your hurry?
- I'll eat my hat
- Keep it under your hat
- Keep your hat on
- Not just a hat rack
- Old hat
- Pass the hat

- Pull more tricks out of your hat
- Pull out of your hat
- Raise your hat
- Ready at the drop of a hat
- Throw your hat in the ring
- Tip your hat
- Pull off a hat trick
- Hats off to you
- Hold on to your hat!
- Wear many hats
- Wear two hats
- Mad as a hatter
- Hem and haw
- Knickers in a knot
- Strait-laced
- Tough as leather
- Assume the mantle
- Mix and match
- The naked truth
- Beat the pants off him
- Bossy pants
- Caught with your pants down
- Charm the pants off him
- Done by the seat of my pants
- Fancy-pants
- Get a kick in the pants
- Liar, liar, pants on fire
- Put on your big-boy pants
- Put your pants on one leg at a time

- Scared out of my pants
- Shaking in your pants
- A smarty-pants

Hold on to your hat!

- Sue the pants off you
- Clutch your pearls
- Pearls of wisdom
- Pin it on that
- A platform issue
- Have him in your pocket
- It's pocket change
- Stay in the pocket
- A pocketbook issue
- Deep pockets
- Line your own pockets
- Press forward
- Pull it together
- A pullover
- Hold the purse strings
- Loosen your purse strings
- Power of the purse

- The purse distribution
- Tighten the purse strings
- Cut the ribbon
- Cut to ribbons
- Put a ring on it
- The ringleader
- Let it rip
- Sartorial splendor
- Scarf down
- A seamless change
- Bursting at the seams
- Coming apart at the seams
- Not too shabby
- Sheer agony
- He'd give you the shirt off his back

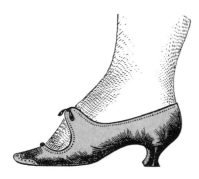

If the shoe fits

- In like a dirty shirt
- Keep your shirt on
- Lose his shirt
- He's a stuffed shirt
- Shirts versus skins

- Comfortable as an old shoe
- The old soft-shoe
- If the shoe fits
- Now the shoe is on the other foot
- An old-fashioned shoe-leather campaign
- A shoe-leather reporter
- Waiting for the other shoe to drop
- White-shoe law firm
- Shoehorn it in
- Big shoes to fill
- Goody two-shoes
- Put yourself in my shoes
- Walk a mile in his shoes
- On a shoestring
- Shopaholic
- Keep your shorts on
- Hit the silk
- A silk purse out of a sow's ear
- Smooth as silk
- Skirt around
- Something up your sleeve
- Laugh up your sleeve
- Wear it on my sleeve
- Wear your heart on your sleeve
- Time to roll up your sleeves
- A sock for every old slipper
- Put a sock in it
- A sock hop

Put yourself in my shoes

- Sock it away
- Sock it to 'em
- Knock your socks off
- Pull your socks up
- A stitch in time saves nine
- Don't cramp my style
- Going out in style
- All over him like a cheap suit
- In your birthday suit
- An empty suit
- Suit up
- Suit your fancy
- The men in gray suits
- Suits me
- To be tailor-made
- Receive tailored information
- A common thread
- Hanging by a thread

- A tough needle to thread

- Threadbare

- Like threading a needle

- Tie the knot

- Tie up loose ends

- Tie yourself up in knots

- Fit to be tied

- Tied up

- Sever ties with

- On trend

- A trend-setter

- The veil of secrecy

- Play it close to the vest

- In vogue

- Warp and woof

- None the worse for wear

- Ready-to-wear

- Wear and tear

- You wear it well

- Wear out your welcome

- A wedge issue

- All wool and a yard wide

- Dyed-in-the-wool

- Pull the wool over their eyes

- Worn out

- Keep it under wraps

- Spin a yarn

Tie yourself up in knots

FOOD & COOKING

1.

2.

3.

- Bread-and-butter issue
- The breadbasket
- The breadwinner
- Break bread
- Cast your bread upon the waters
- Crying with a loaf of bread under your arm
- The greatest thing since sliced bread
- On the breadline
- It's our bread and butter
- A bun in the oven
- Carb-load
- He's a crumb
- Crumble under pressure
- The upper crust
- Rolling in dough
- The whole enchilada
- All the fixin's
- Go against the grain
- Not a grain of truth to it
- Muffin top
- Noodle it over
- Use your noodle
- A wet noodle
- Feeling your oats
- Flat as a pancake
- A compliment sandwich
- The sandwich generation
- Throw spaghetti at the wall
- Let's blow this taco stand

- Give a toast
- You're toast
- Toasty warm
- That's a wrap
- It's like butter
- Butter him up
- Butter wouldn't melt in her mouth
- Butterfingers
- Soft as butter
- The big cheese
- The cheese slipped off the cracker
- Be cheesy
- Cut the cheese
- More holes than Swiss cheese
- Say cheese
- The cream rises to the top
- Cream the other team
- Skim the cream off the top
- He's a bad egg
- Bald as an egg
- Egg him on
- He's a good egg
- Have egg on your face
- Last one in is a rotten egg
- Lay a golden egg
- Lay an egg
- Can't even boil an egg
- One egg short of an omelette
- He's a rotten egg

The apple doesn't fall far from the tree

- Time to break some eggs
- Walk on eggshells
- The apple of my eye
- An apple-polisher
- Apples to apples
- Apples to oranges
- He's a bad apple
- Don't upset the apple cart
- How do you like them apples?
- Polish the apples
- He's a rotten apple
- Take a bite of the apple
- The apple doesn't fall far from the tree
- You only get one bite at the apple
- Criss-cross applesauce

- Go bananas
- Top banana
- The whole banana
- A bite at the cherry
- Cherry on top
- Cherry-pick
- Life is just a bowl of cherries
- Bear fruit
- Bitter fruit
- Forbidden fruit
- Fruit of the poisonous tree
- The fruits of your labor
- Low-hanging fruit
- Make things gel
- Sour grapes
- That's my jam
- Jam someone up
- Jam-packed
- Turn out to be a lemon
- Peach fuzz
- Peachy keen
- She's a real peach
- Pretty as a peach
- Pear-shaped
- Pit against one another
- It's the pits
- A plum assignment
- Blowing raspberries
- A rotten tomato
- A bean counter

- I don't know beans about it
- Full of beans
- He looks like a string bean
- Not worth a bean
- A carrot-and-stick approach
- A carrottop
- Corn-fed
- Cornrows
- A corny joke
- A kernel of hope
- A kernel of truth
- Aw, shucks!
- A hot tamale
- Cool as a cucumber
- Curry favor
- A ginger
- Out of your gourd
- Keen as mustard
- He can't cut the mustard
- Hold the mustard
- Put some mustard on it
- Aw, nuts
- Driving me nuts
- It's an old chestnut
- It pays peanuts
- A tough nut to crack
- That's it in a nutshell
- Know your onions
- Peel the onion
- Like shelling peas

- In a pickle
- Dropped like a hot potato
- Potato, potahto
- Small potatoes
- All vine and no taters
- Salad days

A tough nut to crack

- Open sesame
- Back in the soup
- From soup to nuts
- Soup's on
- Souped up
- I didn't just fall off the turnip truck
- Veg out
- Bring home the bacon
- Full of baloney
- Beef up
- Have a beef with you
- What's your beef?
- Where's the beef?

- It's a nothingburger
- A "butcher boy" play
- Trim the fat
- Good gravy!
- The rest is gravy
- Back to the grind
- Through the meat grinder
- She's a ham
- Ham it up
- Ham-handed
- I'm not chopped liver

- Make mincemeat out of him
- A meat-and-potatoes issue
- A meathead
- Throw red meat to the crowd
- There's no meat on the bone
- A baker's dozen
- A half-baked plan
- Brownie points
- Already baked into the cake
- It's a cakewalk
- The icing on the cake

- Let them eat cake
- Nutty as a fruitcake
- A piece of cake
- Like a kid in a candy store
- Like taking candy from a baby
- All that and a bag of chips
- Dry as a chip
- Caught with your hand in the cookie jar
- Cookie-cutter solution
- A smart cookie
- Toss your cookies
- A tough cookie
- That's the way the cookie crumbles
- To be a crackerjack something
- Get your just desserts
- Time to make the doughnuts
- Doughboy
- Fritter away
- Fudge something
- A honey-do list
- A honey-tongued devil
- Sell like hotcakes
- In mint condition
- A needle in a haystack
- Cutie pie
- Easy as apple pie
- Eat humble pie
- Get a piece of the pie
- A finger in the pie

A "butcher boy" play

- In apple-pie order
- Pie in the sky
- Shut your piehole
- No matter how you slice it
- Let's blow this popsicle stand
- The proof is in the pudding
- Get the scoop
- Scoop it up
- Don't sugar-coat it
- Sugar and spice and everything nice
- A sugar daddy
- A sweet tooth
- Sweet as honey
- Sweet as pie
- Be sweet on someone
- Sweetie pie
- Sweets for the sweet
- Whisper sweet nothings
- A bittersweet moment
- You're in for a treat
- A real treat
- It's plain vanilla
- That's why they make chocolate and vanilla
- Curb your appetite
- Have no appetite for
- Lose your appetite for
- Whet your appetite
- Work up an appetite
- Beat it!

- Beat to a pulp
- Binge-watch
- Champing at the bit
- The breakfast of champions
- Chew him out
- Chew on this
- Chew the cud
- Chew the fat
- Chew the rag
- Chew up the scenery
- Give him something to chew on
- Chow down
- Chop-chop
- A chop shop
- On the chopping block
- Chief cook and bottle-washer
- Cook the books
- Cook up a scheme
- Cook up a storm
- Cook up a story
- I'm cooked
- A pressure cooker
- Too many cooks
- Now you're cooking
- Now you're cooking with gas
- What's cooking?
- Dine and dash
- Eat away at
- Eat crow
- Eat it up

- Eat like a bird
- Eat like a pig
- Eat my dust
- Eat out of the palm of your hand
- Eat the clock
- Eat the frog
- He'll eat you for lunch
- Eat your fill
- Eat your Wheaties!
- He eats like a horse
- Hate to eat and run
- Eat it
- You'll be eaten alive
- Eaten out of house and home
- A picky eater
- Eating like there's no tomorrow
- What's eating you?
- A feast for the eyes
- Neither feast nor famine
- Fed up with someone
- Feed his ego
- Feed off each other
- Feed the meter
- A feeding frenzy
- It's feeding time at the zoo
- Have your fill
- The fat's in the fire
- Out of the frying pan and into the fire
- The flavor of the week

- Put food on the table
- Food for thought
- She's a foodie
- Make a fresh start
- A glutton for punishment
- He was grilled by the police
- Up in my grill
- Rustle up some grub
- Have a hankering for
- Hash out
- Make a hash of it
- The horn of plenty
- That's from hunger
- A hunger strike
- Hungry as a bear
- Hungry for attention
- So hungry I could eat a horse
- Leftovers
- There's no such thing as a free lunch
- Out to lunch
- Made from scratch
- Made to order
- A last meal
- A meal in itself
- A meal ticket
- Meals on wheels
- A stick-to-your-ribs meal
- Thick as mince
- In the mix

- Mix it up
- Nibble around the edges
- Oil and water don't mix
- Pour oil on troubled waters
- Order in
- Pan out
- Tin pan alley
- A flash in the pan
- It was no picnic
- A recipe for disaster
- A recipe for success
- A rotten excuse for a human
- Rotten through and through
- Rotten to the core
- Hit the sauce
- Lost in the sauce
- Sift through
- Simmer down
- Go sour
- An old sourpuss
- Spice things up
- Variety is the spice of life
- Spoiled for choice
- Spoiled rotten
- Spoiler alert
- A greasy spoon
- Go stir-crazy
- Stir things up
- It's on the table
- Whisked away

FOREIGN LANGUAGES

Bon voyage

Amicus curiae

- À la carte
- À la mode
- Ad hoc
- Ad infinitum
- Ad nauseam
- Adieu
- Alma mater
- Amicus curiae
- Après-ski
- Au courant
- Au revoir
- Avant-garde
- Bête noire

- Bon appétit
- Bon mot
- Bon voyage
- Bona fide
- Bonhomie
- Bonjour
- C'est la vie
- Carpe diem
- Carte blanche
- Cause célèbre
- Caveat emptor
- Comme ci, comme ça
- Compos mentis

- Coup d'état
- Coup de grâce
- Crème de la crème
- Cul-de-sac
- Cum laude
- Curriculum vitae
- De facto
- De jure
- De rigueur
- Déjà vu
- Double entendre
- E pluribus unum
- En masse

- Esprit de corps
- Esprit de l'escalier
- Et cetera
- Ex post facto
- Fait accompli
- Faux pas
- Habeas corpus
- Hors d'oeuvre
- In loco parentis
- Ipso facto
- Je ne sais quoi
- Joie de vivre
- Laissez-faire
- Mea culpa
- Merci beaucoup
- Mi casa es su casa
- Modus operandi
- Noblesse oblige
- Nom de guerre
- Nom de plume
- Non sequitur
- Par excellence
- Per diem
- Per se
- Persona non grata
- Pièce de résistance
- Pied-à-terre
- Pro bono
- Pro forma
- Quasi

- Que será, será
- Que te pasa, calabaza?
- Quid pro quo
- Raison d'être
- Rara avis
- Savoir faire
- Sine qua non
- Status quo
- Sui generis
- Tabula rasa
- Terra firma
- Tête-à-tête
- Touché
- Tour de force
- Veni, vidi, vici
- Verbatim
- Vis-à-vis
- Vive la différence
- Volte-face

Tête-à-tête

FUN WORDS & SAYINGS FOR KIDS

1. *Trick or treat* 2. *Flip-flop* 3. *A fairytale ending*

Go beddy-bye

- It ain't over till it's over
- All that gobbledygook
- Alley-oop
- Awesome sauce
- Been there, done that
- Best friends are hard to find because the best ones are already mine
- Betwixt and between
- Boo-boo
- Button your lip
- Bye-bye, French fry
- Chitchat
- Cool beans
- Dilly-dally
- Do-over
- A doozy
- A fairytale ending
- Flimflam artist
- Flip-flop
- Go beddy-bye
- Go ga-ga

- Goody gumdrops
- Hangry
- Hippety-hop
- Howdy-doody
- Hunky-dory
- I'm the boss, applesauce
- I'm rubber, you're glue
- Lickety-split
- A new pair of kicks
- A nincompoop
- A party pooper
- Pinky swear

- Plain old fun
- Pooh-pooh
- Potty mouth
- Pretty please?
- Riffraff
- Shilly-shally
- Skedaddle
- Smartypants
- That's so funny I forgot to laugh
- Sticks and stones
- Tag along
- Tit for tat
- Topsy-turvy
- Trick or treat
- What's shakin', bacon?
- What's the deal, banana peel?
- Whoops-a-daisy
- Wishy-washy
- You break it, you buy it
- Zigzag

Hippety-hop

GAMBLING

1. Don't bet on it   2. Collapse like a house of cards

A few cards short of a deck

- An ace in the hole
- An ace up your sleeve
- Aced it!
- All in
- Ante up
- Up the ante
- Bet dollars to doughnuts
- Bet on the wrong horse
- Bet your bottom dollar
- Bet your life on it
- Don't bet on it
- A safe bet
- All bets are off
- Hedge your bets
- Make bets in a burning house
- Do his bidding
- Bluff your way out
- Call his bluff
- A card-carrying member
- The trump card
- A wild card
- Collapse like a house of cards
- A few cards short of a deck

- Fold your cards
- Hold all the cards
- Lay all your cards on the table
- It's not in the cards
- Play all your cards
- Play your cards right
- Cast your lot
- Take your chances
- You pay your money and you take your chances
- A bargaining chip
- Cash in your chips
- In the chips
- Let the chips fall where they may
- Put all your chips on the table
- When the chips are down
- A crap shoot
- Deal from the bottom of the deck
- Dealer's choice
- Hit me, dealer
- Dealt a bad hand
- Not playing with a full deck

- Stack the deck
- Load the dice
- No dice
- A roll of the dice
- A little dicey
- The die is cast
- Above the fold
- Below the fold
- An opening gambit
- A gamble that paid off
- Take a gamble on
- Play a tough hand
- Hit the jackpot
- Cut your losses
- At odds
- Keep your options open
- Shave the points
- A poker face
- Rake the pot

Let the chips fall where they may

- At risk
- A flight risk
- Risk analysis
- A risk factor
- Risk-averse
- Run the risk
- Take a risk
- A high roller
- Lost in the shuffle
- Shuffle the deck
- Pay off in spades
- Well-stacked
- Have a stake in the game
- Follow suit
- It's not his strong suit
- Tapped out
- He doesn't miss a trick
- That'll do the trick

Tapped out

HEAVEN & HELL

- An angel of mercy
- The City of Angels
- A fallen angel
- Guardian angel
- Listen to your better angels
- She's a little angel
- On the side of the angels
- Where angels fear to tread
- The pearly gates
- For heaven's sake
- It's heaven
- Heaven can wait
- Heaven forbid
- Heaven help us
- Heaven knows
- It's heaven on earth

An angel of mercy

- Heaven-sent
- Heavenly bliss
- A little piece of heaven
- Manna from heaven

- A match made in heaven
- Move heaven and earth
- A slice of heaven
- Thank heaven
- There's a special place in heaven for you
- I thought I'd died and gone to heaven
- Why in heaven's name
- Good heavens!
- Heavens above!
- Heavens no!
- The heavens opened up
- A fool's paradise
- Trouble in paradise
- Utopia
- Valhalla
- Xanadu
- Between heaven and hell
- Damn it!
- Damned if you do, damned if you don't
- Damn with faint praise
- Give a damn
- Dang it!
- I'll be darned!
- Beat the devil at his own game
- Bedevil
- Catch the devil
- He's a crafty devil
- A devil in disguise

- The devil is in the details
- A devil of a job

Heaven-sent

- A devil of a time
- The devil you know is better than the devil you don't
- A devil-may-care attitude
- A devil's bargain
- Full of the devil
- Give the devil his due
- Go to the devil
- He's a handsome devil
- He has the devil to pay
- An idle mind is the devil's playground
- Just for the devil of it
- Make a deal with the devil
- Old as the devil
- Play the devil's advocate

- Raise the devil
- Scare the devil out of him
- Sell your soul to the devil
- Speak of the devil
- The devil incarnate
- What in the devil do you make of this?
- What the devil's gotten into you?
- A harbinger of doom
- A necessary evil
- All hell broke loose
- Sure as hell
- Beat the hell out of him
- Busy as hell
- Catch hell
- It'll be a cold day in hell
- Deals made in hell aren't witnessed by angels
- Do it for the hell of it
- Fight like hell
- The gates of hell
- Get the hell out
- Get the hell out of dodge
- Give 'em hell
- Go to hell in a handbasket
- Go to hell with yourself
- Through hell and back
- To hell and gone
- To be hell-bent on
- Hellfire

- Hell hath no fury like a woman scorned
- Hell no!
- A hell of a mess
- It's hell on earth
- Hell on wheels
- A hell-raiser
- Hell week
- The hell with it
- To hell with them
- Hell's bells
- Hotter than hell
- I'm in hell
- Knocks the hell out of you
- A living hell
- Mad as hell
- A match made in hell
- Not a hope in hell

- He's one hell of a guy
- Pure hell
- Put through hell
- Raise hell
- Raise holy hell
- The road to hell is paved with good intentions
- Rot in hell
- Scare the hell out of me
- Shot to hell
- There'll be hell to pay
- Things going to hell
- Took off like a bat out of hell
- What the hell?
- You don't have a snowball's chance in hell
- What in tarnation is going on here?

Scare the devil out of him

HOT & COLD

Full of hot air

- Beat the heat
- Feel the heat
- Generate a lot of heat and light
- The heat is on
- The heat of the moment
- If you can't take the heat, get out of the kitchen
- In a dead heat
- More heat than light
- Pack heat
- Take some heat
- Turn down the heat
- Turn up the heat
- Full of hot air
- Get it while it's hot
- Heating up
- Hot and bothered
- Hot and heavy
- Hot as a pistol
- Hot as Hades
- A hot mess
- A hot number
- Hot off the presses
- Hot on the case
- Hot on the trail
- Hot on your heels
- A hot shot
- Hot-stove league
- Hot stuff
- A hot temper

- A hot ticket
- A hot tip
- Hot to trot
- A hot topic
- Hot under the collar
- Hot-blooded
- A hot-button issue
- Hotfoot it out of there
- A hothead
- The hotline
- In hot pursuit
- In hot water
- On a hot streak
- On the hot seat
- Piping hot
- Too hot to handle
- It's a scorcher out there
- Raise the temperature
- Keep your seat warm
- Warm and fuzzy
- Warm the cockles of my heart
- Warm up to
- A warmup
- Be chill
- Chill out
- Chilled to the bone
- A chilling effect
- It gives me the chills
- Thrills and chills
- Cast a cold eye on

- Catch a cold
- Cold as ice
- A cold call
- Cold comfort
- Cold hard cash
- A cold one

Cold feet

- A cold send-off
- The cold shoulder
- A cold spell
- A cold sweat
- The cold war
- Cold-blooded
- Coldhearted
- The cold, hard facts
- Come in from the cold
- Down cold
- Cold feet
- Go cold turkey
- Ice cold

Left out in the cold

- In cold blood
- Left out in the cold
- Out cold
- Stop it cold
- Throw cold water on it
- Colder than ice
- Calm, cool, and collected
- That's cool
- Cool down

- Cool it
- Cool your heels
- Cool your jets
- Keep a cool head
- Keep your cool
- Look cool
- Lose your cool
- Let cooler heads prevail

HOUSE & HOME

1. Open doors 2. Knock on doors 3. Camped out on your doorstep

- Bed down
- Bed head
- It's a bed of nails
- Be in bed with someone
- Put it to bed

Strange bedfellows

- Put to bed
- Strange bedfellows
- A bedroom community
- Bedroom eyes
- Embed with
- Blanket approval
- A blanket statement
- A security blanket
- A wet blanket
- A light bulb going off in one's head
- Bunk down for the night
- Cabin fever
- Get called on the carpet
- Carpetbagger
- Break the glass ceiling
- Hit the ceiling

- Chair a committee
- Fold like a lawn chair
- I nearly fell off my chair
- Play first chair
- An armchair critic
- An armchair general
- Beat the clock
- Can't turn back the clock
- I'll clean your clock
- The clock is ticking
- Clock out
- The clock strikes twelve
- Kill the clock
- Off the clock
- On the clock
- Punch the clock
- Race against the clock
- Roll back the clock
- Speed up the clock
- Get clocked
- It's going like clockwork
- Come out of the closet
- Closeted away
- A cottage industry
- A couch doctor
- Couch it in kind words
- A couch potato
- From cradle to grave
- Rob the cradle
- Pull back the curtain

- It's curtains for you
- Give yourself a little cushion
- A den of iniquity
- Dish it out
- He can dish it out, but he can't take it
- Treat like a dishrag
- At your disposal
- A backdoor approach
- Close the door on something
- Don't let the door hit you on the way out
- The door is always open
- Door-to-door
- Get in through the back door
- Get something out the door
- Leave the door open
- An open-door policy
- A revolving door
- Show him the door
- Shut the front door
- Slam the door in his face
- Treated like a doormat
- Behind closed doors
- Knock on doors
- Open doors
- They're breaking the doors down
- Camped out on your doorstep
- Place blame on one's doorstep
- Circling the drain

- Down the drain
- Top-drawer
- Don't dwell on it
- Set off a false alarm
- Hit the fan
- A fork in the road
- Fork it over
- Fork out
- Part of the furniture
- Gaslight someone
- A gate-crasher
- Get out of the gate early
- Keeper of the gate
- A safe haven
- Bring it home
- Charity begins at home
- Come home to roost
- Don't leave home without it
- Her home is like a dollhouse
- A home away from home
- Home-field advantage
- Home free
- Home is where the heart is
- Home is where you hang your hat
- Home sweet home
- In the homestretch
- It hits close to home
- Keep the home fires burning
- Make yourself at home

- Romp home
- There's no place like home
- You can't go home again
- A homebody
- Homegrown terrorists
- A homewrecker
- Get hosed
- Bring the house down

Get hosed

- A flophouse
- A full house
- A boardinghouse reach
- The house always wins
- House poor
- In the big house
- Like a house on fire
- Madam of the house
- It's on the house
- Open house
- Play to a packed house
- Play to an empty house
- Playing with house money
- Put your house in order
- Rocked the house

- Roughhouse
- A row house
- A household name
- A golden key can open any door
- A key to success
- Under lock and key
- Keyed up
- Knickknacks
- He's not the sharpest knife in the drawer
- Have a lock on it
- Lock it up
- Lock something down
- On lockdown
- Locked in
- Locked out
- Get off the mat
- Go to the mat for him
- Fun-house mirror
- The mirror image
- Mirror someone
- House of mirrors
- Mortgage your future
- Know every nook and cranny
- Cool as the other side of the pillow
- Pillow talk
- As if he owns the place
- Crash at my place
- A full plate
- Close quarters

- Tight quarters
- Off your rocker
- All under one roof
- Through the roof
- Hit the roof
- To live under my roof
- Raise the roof
- The roof is caving in
- A roof over your head
- Make room
- The powder room
- There's no room at the inn
- Wiggle room
- Cut a rug
- Lie like a rug
- Pull the rug out from under him
- The best seat in the house
- Sew up a deal
- Shack up
- Put it on the shelf
- Shelf life
- Fly off the shelves
- Jump into the shower
- Sent to the showers
- Everything but the kitchen sink
- Sink in
- Born with a silver spoon in his mouth
- Gag me with a spoon
- Spoon-fed

- Up the down staircase
- The three-legged stool
- Fall between two stools
- A stovepipe pattern
- Bring something to the table
- A deal made under the table
- Have a place at the table
- Have a seat at the table
- A kitchen-table issue
- Kitchen-table politics
- Doesn't bring much to the table
- Nothing is off the table
- Ready to come to the table
- Set the table
- Table an issue
- Table scraps
- Table the motion
- Turn the tables on
- Cross the threshold
- What makes you tick
- Takes a licking and keeps on ticking
- Tied to his mother's apron strings
- Throw in the towel
- Living in an ivory tower
- A tower of strength
- Tower over
- Come in over the transom
- Right as a trivet
- Hit a wall

A clean sweep

- A hole in the wall
- It fits like the paper on the wall
- A window of time
- The ash heap of history
- Give the brush-off
- Clean house
- A clean sweep
- Clean up
- Come clean
- A member of the clean-plate club
- Squeaky-clean
- Cleaned out
- Taken to the cleaners
- Clogged up
- Comb through it
- Went over with a fine-toothed comb
- Dull as dishwater
- Hung out to dry
- A dustup
- The dustbin of history

- Done and dusted
- The fuzz
- Garbage in, garbage out
- Ready for the garbage heap
- Iron out the details
- Iron out the kinks
- Iron out the wrinkles
- Launder money
- Air your dirty laundry in public
- A laundry list of complaints
- Mop it up
- Mop the floor with you
- Move the needle
- Needle him
- On pins and needles
- Neat as a pin
- Pin down
- Pin him down
- Pin your hopes on
- Put a pin in it
- Spit and polish
- Scrub the data
- It's all sewn up
- Spick-and-span
- The fun sponge
- Take the starch out of you
- In stitches
- Sweep it under the rug
- In a vacuum
- It doesn't wash

- It will all come out in the wash
- It's a wash
- Whitewash the problem
- All washed up
- The great unwashed
- A washout
- Waste away
- Put through the wringer

Air your dirty laundry in public

IN & OUT

• All in all

• All in good fun

• In the aughts

• Bring it in

• Closing in

• Clue someone in

• Draw in

• Factor in

• Fill in

• Have an in

• Have it in for someone

• Hold in

• Home in on

• In a crunch

• In a flap about something

• In a quandary

• In a snit

• In a tizzy

• In and of itself

• In cahoots

• In depth

• In its own right

• In on something

• In person

• In store

• In the buff

• In the grand scheme of things

• In the gutter

• In the main

• In the middle of nowhere

A sit-in

• In the neighborhood

• In touch with

• Lay into

• Lean in

• Left in the lurch

• Pass out

• Phase in

• Plug in

• Pop in

• It's popping in here

• Put him in his place

• Roll out

• Roll out the red carpet

• Rub it in

• See someone in

• A shoo-in

• A sit-in

• Soak it all up

• Take it all in

• Take part in

• Take pride in

• Taken in

• Tap in

• Tapped into

• Throw in

• A tie-in

• Tuck in

• What's in it for me?

• Zoom in on

• In and out

• The ins and outs

• Bang it out

• Borne out

• Break out

• A breakout hit

• Bring out the best

• Carry out

• Carve out

• Clean someone out

• Clear out

• Close out

• Cut out

- Dole out
- I don't get out much
- Drop out
- A dropout
- Eke out
- Fallen out of favor
- Flat out
- Freak out
- Get out from under
- Get out of something
- Get out of the way of
- Given an out
- Grind it out
- Hang out
- Have a falling-out
- Hold out
- I'm out
- Knock out
- Know inside out
- Lash out
- Last in, first out
- Let it all hang out
- Make out
- Map out
- Max out
- Miss out
- On the outs
- Opt out
- Out and about
- Out in the open

Have a falling-out

- Out of it
- Out of nowhere
- Out of place
- Out of the ordinary
- Out of the question
- Out of turn
- Out of whack
- An out-and-out lie
- Outdo yourself
- Over and out
- Parse out
- Phase out
- Pluck out
- Plug out
- Point out
- Pull out all the stops
- Put him out on the street
- Rub someone out
- Seek out
- Sell out
- Set it out
- Set out

- Shut out
- Skip out
- Snap out of it
- Sort out
- Spit it out
- Spit out
- Stake out
- Stand out
- Suss it out
- Swap out
- Take a hit out on someone
- Take him out
- Take it out on
- Take the easy way out
- Test out
- Throw out
- Tough it out
- Try out
- Weirded out
- Wipe out
- Work it out

THE LAW

1.

2.

1. Last pitch to the jury   2. Tell it to the judge

- Aid and abet
- Alert the authorities
- Make out like bandits
- Behind bars
- Lay blame
- Get busted
- Cease and desist
- An escape clause
- In the clink
- A con man
- Cop a plea
- Cop an attitude
- Cop out
- Good cop, bad cop
- Like the Keystone Kops
- Undercover work
- A crackdown on crime
- Crime doesn't pay
- It's not the crime, it's the cover-up
- Partners in crime
- The perfect crime
- Let the punishment fit the crime
- True crime
- Hardened criminal
- A two-bit crook
- Crooked as the day is long
- Cuff 'em
- Under false pretenses
- Pull a fast one

- Fess up
- Go scot-free
- Guilt by association
- Guilty as sin
- A guilty conscience
- Innocent until proven guilty
- A holdup
- What's the holdup?
- It keeps me honest
- A get-out-of-jail-free card
- The joint
- Take it on the lam

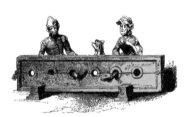

Let the punishment fit the crime

- A lineup
- Lock him up and throw away the key
- Locked up
- Let loose
- An ulterior motive
- Get away with murder
- Murder and mayhem
- In the pokey
- Life imprisonment
- Take no prisoners
- Pull over

- A bum rap
- Have a rap sheet
- Take the rap
- Read the riot act
- She's a riot
- There's a new sheriff in town
- Thrown in the slammer
- A stakeout
- Steal a kiss
- Steal away
- This is a stickup!
- The usual suspects
- There's no honor among thieves
- It takes a thief
- Thick as thieves
- Like thieves in the night
- A true threat
- Do time
- Serve time
- Under the auspices of someone
- Appear before the bench
- Lodge a complaint
- Court of last resort
- Court of public opinion
- A friend of the court
- Have your day in court
- Hold court
- May it please the court
- Order in the court!
- See you in court

- Come courting
- Deemed necessary
- The benefit of the doubt
- Prima facie evidence
- Without a shred of evidence
- It's evident that
- The facts speak for themselves
- Get the facts wrong
- Fair enough
- Through no fault of my own
- Gavel-to-gavel coverage
- Pass the gavel
- Put your imprimatur on something
- Both judge and jury
- I'll be the judge of that
- Tell it to the judge
- You be the judge
- Judgment day
- A judgment call
- A lapse in judgment
- Pass judgment
- A rush to judgment
- Snap judgment
- A hung jury
- The jury is still out
- Last pitch to the jury
- Just cause
- Brought to justice
- Do it justice

- Jersey justice
- Justice is blind
- Justice is served
- No justice, no peace
- Rough justice
- Seek justice
- Swift justice
- A travesty of justice
- A class-action lawsuit
- A moot point
- It's null and void
- Foolproof
- Prove beyond a reasonable doubt
- Proving grounds
- No good deed goes unpunished
- Balance the scales
- Take the stand
- I could have sworn that
- A bench trial
- On trial
- Trial and error
- Trial by fire
- A trial run
- The trials and tribulations of
- The truth will set you free
- Know the whys and wherefores
- Against your will
- Will it
- An eyewitness account

- Flip the witness
- Witness it firsthand
- Reach an agreement
- Above the law
- Equal before the law
- A brush with the law
- In trouble with the law
- The law of averages
- Law of the land
- He's a law unto himself
- A law with no teeth
- Lay down the law
- Letter of the law
- Possession is nine-tenths of the law
- Spirit of the law
- Take the law into your own hands
- Lawyer up
- A legal eagle
- A legal wrinkle
- It's legit
- Find a loophole
- Right of way
- The right to bear arms
- Squatter's rights
- Within your rights
- No hard-and-fast rule
- The rule of law
- Bend the rules
- Rules of engagement

LIFE & DEATH

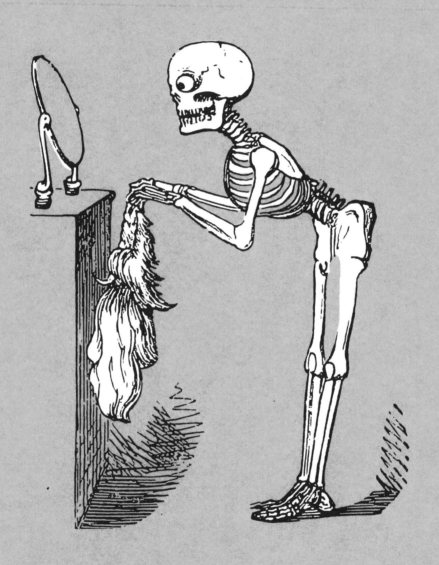

A killer view

- Born again
- There's one born every minute
- I wasn't born yesterday
- A humdrum existence
- Breathe new life into something
- Bring to life
- Don't let life pass you by
- The elixir of life
- Every walk of life
- A fact of life
- For life
- For the life of me
- Get a life
- Get on with your life
- The good life
- Guard it with your life
- A hard-knock life
- The high life
- Hold on for dear life
- Larger than life
- Lay down your life
- Life begins at forty
- Life coach
- Life expectancy
- Life force
- A life-form
- A life lesson
- The life of Riley
- The life of the party
- Life partner

- A life principle
- Life skills
- Your life story
- Life-sized
- Life-threatening
- Live a charmed life
- Live a fantasy life
- Live a full life
- A lowlife
- Make a life for yourself
- Not on your life
- On life support

Alive and kicking

- One life to live
- The prime of your life
- Pro-life

- Public life
- Put your life on the line
- Quality of life
- The right to life
- Set for life
- Slice of life
- The span of life
- Spring to life
- Take life as it comes
- Take on a life of its own
- Take your life in your hands
- Throw someone a life jacket
- The time of your life
- Tiptoe through life
- True life
- A way of life
- Man the lifeboats
- A lifeline
- A lifesaver
- A lifestyle
- In another lifetime
- Not in your lifetime
- Once in a lifetime
- It's the little things
- Alive and kicking
- Do it live
- Live a little
- As I live and breathe
- Live and learn
- Live and let live

- Live beyond your means
- Live for the moment
- Live free or die
- Live from hand to mouth
- Live happily ever after
- Live high on the hog
- Live in a bubble

- Live large
- Live life to the fullest
- Live like there's no tomorrow
- Live off someone
- Live off the fat of the land
- Live on the edge
- Live on top of us

- Live out of your suitcase
- Live to tell the tale
- Live to regret it
- Live to the hilt
- A live wire
- Live with it
- Live within your means
- You'll never live it down
- Outlive
- We've got a live one
- Short-lived
- Livestream
- Assisted living
- Clean living
- In living memory
- The land of the living
- Living arrangement
- Living in sin
- A living legend
- Living proof
- Living quarters
- Living space
- A living thing
- A living wage
- It's a marathon, not a sprint
- A needle in a haystack
- Wanted dead or alive
- A matter of life and death
- Live by the sword, die by the sword

Live in a bubble

- Go home in a box
- Buried in the stacks
- Buried in work

Roll over and play dead

- To bury the lede
- Give someone the creeps
- Better off dead
- Brain dead
- Carry some dead weight
- Chivalry is dead
- Dead ahead
- Dead aim
- Dead air
- Dead and gone
- Dead asleep
- Dead at the hands of
- Dead bolt
- Dead broke
- Dead calm
- A dead dog
- Dead giveaway
- Dead in the water
- Dead letter
- Dead lift
- Dead man walking

- Dead meat
- Dead on arrival
- Dead on your feet
- Dead presidents
- Dead right
- A dead ringer
- Dead set against it
- Dead slow
- Dead space
- Dead tired
- Dead to the world
- Dead wrong
- Dead-on
- Don't beat a dead horse
- Drop-dead gorgeous
- Good and dead
- Got him dead to rights
- Half-dead
- Knock 'em dead
- Left for dead
- More dead than alive
- Over my dead body
- Raise the dead
- Roll over and play dead
- Wake the dead
- I wouldn't be caught dead
- A deadbeat
- At death's door
- Bored to death
- A brush with death

- Cheat death
- Death metal
- You'll be the death of me
- A death sentence
- A death trap
- A death wish
- Die a natural death
- Die a slow death
- A fate worse than death
- Flirt with death
- Fresh to death
- Look like death warmed over
- Near death
- A near-death experience
- On death row
- Scared to death
- Sound the death knell for
- Sudden death
- Tested to death
- Tickled to death
- Till death do us part
- The valley of death
- On your deathbed
- Die a thousand deaths
- Curl up and die
- Die away
- Die back
- Die laughing
- Die off
- Die on the vine

- Die out
- Die penniless
- Die with your boots on
- Do or die
- I will die if something happens
- Who died and made you boss?
- Who died and made you god?
- A die-hard
- Dig your own grave
- A dying art
- Dying to get into
- Dying to know
- Your dying wish
- It's not a hill worth dying on
- Until my dying day
- A dead end
- A dead-end job
- The end is near
- The end of days
- End of story
- It's your funeral
- Gallows humor
- Ghost someone
- A ghost town
- Give up the ghost
- Not a ghost of a chance
- Gone but not forgotten
- Beyond the grave
- Carry it to your grave
- Don't stomp on the grave of

- It will put me in the grave
- Send him to an early grave
- Turn over in your grave
- The graveyard shift
- Whistling past the graveyard
- Give someone grief
- A trip to heaven
- Catch and kill
- Go in for the kill
- Kill 'em with kindness
- Kill it
- Kill me now
- Kill the bill
- Kill the story
- A license to kill
- Overkill
- You killed it
- A killer view
- A killer workout
- Killer-diller
- You're killing me
- Make a killing
- Don't be a killjoy
- Even if it kills me
- Finish dead last
- Last but not least
- A last chance
- The last frontier
- Last gasp
- The last hurrah

- Save the best for last
- Live up to
- Mow down
- Pass away
- Pass into the great beyond
- Pass to the other side
- Perish the thought
- Phantom limb
- Phantom pain
- The grim reaper
- Final resting place
- Raise the specter of
- Scared stiff
- Cheat the worms

LIGHT & DARK

Beginning to see the light

- Bright-eyed and bushy-tailed
- The best and the brightest
- At the break of dawn
- At the crack of dawn
- Dawn on you
- Something by day
- Begin to see daylight
- Burn daylight
- In broad daylight
- Put some daylight between us
- Scare the living daylights out of him
- A gleam in your eye
- All sweetness and light
- At first light
- A beacon of light
- See the facts in a different light
- Beginning to see the light
- Bring to light
- Come to light
- An enlightening experience
- Faster than the speed of light
- A guiding light
- In light of
- It won't see the light of day
- Jump the light
- Knock someone's lights out
- Let there be light
- Light at the end of the tunnel
- Light him up

- The light of my life
- Light on your feet
- Light up
- Light years away
- The lights are on but no one's home
- Lights! Camera! Action!
- Make light of
- Not a shred of light
- Out like a light

Light at the end of the tunnel

- Put it in a new light
- Put yourself in the best light
- See the light
- Shed light on the subject
- Shown in a bad light
- Trip the light fantastic

- Lighten up
- Lighten your load
- To put it lightly
- Take it lightly
- In the limelight
- He's lit
- Lit up like a Christmas tree
- Live in his own shadow
- Rise and shine
- In the twinkle of an eye
- When he was just a twinkle in his mother's eye
- Paint a dark picture
- The dark ages
- A dark comedy
- A dark day
- A dark horse
- A dark moment
- It's his dark side
- The dark web
- A deep, dark secret
- Go dark
- Go over to the dark side
- Kept in the dark
- Left in the dark
- It's a shot in the dark
- A stab in the dark
- Take a dark view
- Tall, dark, and handsome
- That was dark

Cast a big shadow

- Cast a shadow over his chances
- Come out of the shadows
- In the shadow of someone
- A lasting shadow
- Left a shadow of a man
- Overshadowed by someone
- Shadowboxing
- A shadow of his former self
- Like something out of the twilight zone
- Twilight years

- Be totally in the dark
- Whistling in the dark
- It's always darkest just before the dawn
- It's always darkest under the lighthouse
- Darkest hour
- Fade away
- Not fade away
- In the dead of night

- A night out on the town
- Something by night
- Made in the shade
- Shade the truth
- Shady
- Throw shade
- Afraid of your own shadow
- Beyond a shadow of a doubt
- Cast a big shadow

LITERARY

On the same page

- Fill in the blanks
- Book 'em
- Called every name in the book
- Close the book on
- A closed book
- Do it by the book
- Have your nose in a book
- His life is like an open book
- Not in my book
- The oldest trick in the book
- Play by the book
- Take a leaf out of his book
- Take a page from his book
- Throw the book at him
- Use every trick in the book
- Write the book on
- Balance the books
- Fudge the books
- In someone's good books
- One for the books
- Wipe it off the books
- A bookworm
- Cite chapter and verse
- The final chapter is yet to be written
- Character assassination
- Character is destiny
- A shady character
- Cover to cover
- Ink a deal

- A walking encyclopedia
- An epic fail
- It was epic
- Separate fact from fiction
- Truth is stranger than fiction
- Act before the ink is dry
- Get inked
- Have an inkling
- It's legendary
- Follow instructions to the letter
- Letter-perfect
- Stick to the letter of the law
- Have a lot of letters after your name
- A man of letters
- Dot the i's and cross the t's
- Fit to a "t"
- Have it down to a "t"
- Literary license
- Mystery solved
- Note to self
- Take note of
- Compare notes
- Be open to something
- Jump off the page
- On the same page
- A real page-turner
- Turn a page
- Look good on paper
- Not worth the paper it's printed on

- Paper over
- A poison-pen letter
- Put pen to paper
- With the stroke of a pen
- Penned in
- Turn a phrase
- Plot against
- The plot thickens
- Poetic justice
- Poetic license
- Wax poetic
- Poetry in motion
- Stop the presses
- Able to read people
- An easy read
- A good read
- A quick read
- Read 'em and weep
- Read between the lines
- Read his mind
- Read into something
- Read the fine print
- Read up on
- A sweet read
- Well-read
- Bumper-sticker rhetoric
- Neither rhyme nor reason
- Riddled with
- Stiff sentence
- That's another story

- The backstory
- A Cinderella story
- Get the story straight
- A heartwarming story
- The inside story
- That's a likely story
- Make up a story
- A sob story
- The story has legs
- The story of my life
- It's the same old story
- A whale of a story
- What's the story?
- A storybook ending
- Stranger things have happened
- Spin a tale
- Term limits
- In no uncertain terms
- Terms of endearment
- Take out of context
- A buzzword
- Can't get a word in edgewise
- A dirty word
- Find the right word
- Get the word out
- Go back on your word
- Hang on your every word
- You have my word
- Have the last word
- Hold him to his word

- Just say the word
- Keep your word
- The magic word
- A man of his word
- May I have a word with you?
- Mum's the word
- My word is my bond
- Only as good as your word
- The operative word
- Put in a good word
- Send word
- Spread the word
- Stick to your word
- Take him at his word
- Upon my word
- What's the good word?
- Word for word
- Word gets around
- A word of advice
- The word on the street
- Word perfect
- Word salad
- A word to the wise
- Word up
- At a loss for words
- Choke on your own words
- Choose your words wisely
- Eat your words
- Famous last words
- Hard to put into words

- A way with words
- Have words
- In other words
- Mark my words
- Measure your words carefully
- Mince words
- Never be lost for words
- A play on words
- There are no words to describe it
- Walk your words back
- A woman of few words
- Words fail me
- Words of wisdom
- Words to that effect
- Nothing to write home about
- Write him off
- Write it up
- Write up
- Put it in writing
- See the writing on the wall
- Disaster written all over it
- Written all over your face
- Written in plain English
- Written in the stars
- Written off
- Written up
- That's all she wrote

LOVE & KISSES

Love nest

- Kiss and make up
- Kiss and tell
- Kiss away the tears
- Kiss his ass

- Kissing cousins
- All's fair in love and war
- Fall in love
- For love or money
- For the love of
- Free love
- To know him is to love him
- Love at first sight
- Love child

- Love match
- Love nest
- The love of my life
- A love triangle
- Love trumps hate
- Love will find a way
- A love-hate relationship
- Madly in love
- Make love not war

Lovestruck

- Kiss it goodbye
- It's the kiss of death
- Kiss off
- Kiss the ring
- Kiss up to
- Do you kiss your mother with that mouth?
- Sun-kissed
- Right in the kisser!

- Love conquers all
- A love fest
- Love handles
- Love is blind
- Love it or leave it
- Love knot
- Love life
- Love makes the world go 'round

- No love lost between them
- Not for love or money
- Tough love
- True love
- It's better to have loved and lost
- Take a lover
- Lovers' quarrel
- Lovestruck

- Lovey-dovey
- Left at the altar
- Make a clean break
- Always a bridesmaid, never a bride
- A bromance
- Take care of
- Have a crush on someone
- Yes, dear
- Dump someone
- Flirting with disaster
- The honeymoon is over
- Honeymoon period
- They're an item
- To my liking
- I love you to the moon and back
- Misery loves company
- Lust after
- Wanderlust
- A left-handed marriage
- A marriage of convenience
- Marrying up
- Meet your match
- A perfect match
- Play matchmaker
- Follow your passion
- Pop the question
- An on-and-off relationship
- Shy away from
- Snuggle up

- Have a soft spot for
- A sweetheart deal
- Take kindly to something
- Take to someone
- I'm not wedded to it

A bromance

LUCK

A lucky devil

- By any chance
- The chance of a lifetime
- Chance upon
- Don't leave it to chance
- Destined for greatness
- A rendezvous with destiny
- The master of your own fate
- Seal someone's fate
- Tempt fate
- A twist of fate
- A reversal of fortune
- The wheel of fortune
- It's a given
- As good as it gets
- Too good to be true
- Don't jinx me
- As luck would have it
- Beginner's luck
- Best of luck
- Better luck next time
- Don't press your luck
- Don't push your luck
- Down on your luck
- Dumb luck
- A hard luck story
- In luck
- Just my luck
- Lady luck
- The luck of the devil
- The luck of the draw

- The luck of the Irish
- Luck out
- My luck ran out
- No such luck
- One for good luck
- Out of luck
- Potluck
- Rotten luck

Born under a lucky star

- A run of bad luck
- A stroke of good luck
- Tough luck
- Try your luck
- Born under a lucky star
- Happy-go-lucky
- A lucky break

- A lucky devil
- A lucky dog
- A lucky streak
- Thank your lucky stars
- Lose your mojo
- Against all odds
- Beat the odds
- Lay odds
- Odds are
- The odds are against you
- The odds-on favorite
- Raise the stakes
- The stakes are high
- Sure thing
- A sure thing
- Bode well

MEASURE & SIZE

On your high horse

Follow a higher calling

- At the high end
- High hopes
- High maintenance
- High noon
- It's high time
- Left high and dry
- On a high
- On your high horse
- Follow a higher calling
- When they go low, we go high
- Feeling low
- How can you sink so low?
- Keep a low profile
- Lay low
- A low blow
- A peg too low
- As far as
- By far
- Far afield

- Far be it from me
- A far cry from
- Far from the finish line
- Far from the truth
- The far side
- Far-fetched
- Few and far between
- Go too far
- So far, so good
- I trust him about as far as I can throw him
- So near and yet so far
- Draw near
- In the near future
- Near and dear
- Near beer
- A near miss
- Be near to
- Near to my heart
- Near term

- At close range
- Close at hand
- Close by
- Close call
- Close combat
- A close fight
- A close shave
- Close the gap
- Close-cropped
- Close, but no cigar
- Cut it close
- Draw close
- Be close with
- Too close for comfort
- Ready for your close-up
- Caught short
- Come up short
- Don't sell yourself short
- Down to the short strokes

- Fall short
- Get the short end of the stick
- Get short shrift
- In short order
- On short notice
- Short and sweet
- Shorthanded
- Short-listed
- Take a shortcut
- He's a tall drink of water
- It's a tall order
- Tell a tall tale
- At long last
- Go long
- In the long run
- The long and short of it
- It's a long road back
- To make a long story short
- My long-lost . . .
- Not long for this world
- Fat chance
- It ain't over until the fat lady sings
- Be the heavy
- Have a thick hide
- In the thick of it
- Pour it on thick
- Be thick
- A wide place in the road
- Give a wide berth

- Lean and mean
- Lean, mean fighting machine
- A narrow escape
- Narrow the gap
- Go skinny-dipping
- Skinny as a toothpick
- A skinny minnie
- What's the skinny?
- Slim chance
- Slim down
- Slim pickings
- My patience is wearing thin
- A razor-thin margin
- Spread yourself too thin
- Stretched too thin
- Thin as a rail
- Thin on top
- Walk a thin line
- Wear thin
- Get ahead
- Get ahead of oneself
- Press ahead
- Pull ahead
- It's beyond me
- Beyond my ken
- Beyond the pale
- Get it over with
- Over the long haul
- Above it all
- A notch above

- Rise above
- Above average
- Below average
- Balance out
- Hanging in the balance
- Between you, me, and the lamppost
- Go off the deep end
- In deep
- In deep trouble
- In deep water
- Out of your depth
- Go the distance
- Keep your distance
- A long-distance relationship
- By almost every measure
- In large measure
- The measure of a man
- Measure up
- One for good measure
- A stopgap measure
- Take his measure
- A measured response
- Guesstimate
- It's a reach
- Within reach
- Scale back
- Scale down
- Scale up
- Tip the scale

- Cut down to size
- Pick on someone your own size
- Size someone up
- Size up the competition
- Size up the problem
- Try this on for size
- Weigh a ton
- Weigh in
- Weigh your options
- Carry your own weight
- Collapse under its own weight
- Give it added weight
- He carries little weight
- A heavyweight
- A lightweight
- Not pulling his weight
- Throw your weight around
- Throw your weight behind
- With every ounce of my being
- Extract a pound of flesh
- Pound for pound
- Give you an inch and you'll take a mile
- Inch your way into
- Know every inch
- Refuse to budge an inch
- A mile a minute
- A miss is as good as a mile
- Get mileage out of
- In dribs and drabs

Step it up a notch

- At the very least
- Just a smidge
- Enough already
- Enough is enough
- Enough said
- Step it up a notch
- Take it down a notch
- Have some left
- Marginal at best
- A happy medium
- It's just so-so
- Caught in the middle
- Meet in the middle
- The middle of the road
- I couldn't care less
- Less is more
- The more the merrier
- There's plenty more where that came from

- Make whole
- Be extra
- Filled to the brim
- The full monty
- Full of bull
- Full of empty promises
- He's full of himself
- Full of it
- Full tilt
- Go to great lengths
- For the greater good
- A load on you
- The best of a bad lot
- It leaves a lot to be desired
- A lot of bunk
- A lot of good that did
- To the max
- Too much of a good thing

MEDICAL & HEALTH

1.

2.

3.

1. In sickness and in health 2. Choose your poison 3. Lick your wounds

- Agonize over
- Prolong the agony
- It's good for what ails you
- An ambulance chaser
- Baby bump
- A band-aid solution
- It's bedlam!
- A good bedside manner
- Couldn't be better
- Never been better
- Bleeding cash
- A bleeding-heart liberal
- Stop the bleeding
- Have blood on your hands
- Out for blood
- Scream bloody murder
- From the bowels of the earth
- Brain drain
- It's not brain surgery
- A chance to catch your breath
- Don't hold your breath
- Don't waste your breath
- In the same breath
- Save your breath
- Take a deep breath
- Take one's breath away
- Waiting with bated breath
- Breathe a sigh of relief
- Breathe easier
- Not a moment to breathe

- Take a breather
- Give him breathing room
- A breathtaking view
- A cancer on
- Cancer sticks
- Get a checkup
- With child
- Comfort the afflicted, and afflict the comfortable
- Make only a cosmetic change
- Cough up the money
- Crack under pressure
- Funny as a crutch
- The cure is worse than the disease
- Clinically dead
- Walking dead
- Feel disjointed
- What's up, doc?
- Doctor it up
- Doctor knows best
- Doctor's orders!
- Is there a doctor in the house?
- Just what the doctor ordered
- A spin doctor
- Drug of choice
- Feel out of sorts
- Not feeling up to it
- Not feeling well
- Not feeling yourself
- Fever pitch

- Under a gag order
- A germ of an idea
- Do more harm than good
- Do no harm
- A splitting headache
- Heal with time
- Healing your wounds
- A clean bill of health
- A health nut
- In the best of health
- Nursed back to health
- A picture of health
- Healthy as a horse
- A healthy disregard
- Hemorrhaging money
- Hobble around
- Hobbled
- It can't hurt to try
- Hurt someone's pride
- It hurts like the dickens
- To fall ill
- Ill at ease
- Add insult to injury
- The inmates are running the asylum
- A jaundiced eye
- Go under the knife
- Laugh yourself sick
- Take your lumps
- It's bad medicine

- Laughter is the best medicine
- Practice preventative medicine
- It's strong medicine to take
- Take your medicine
- On the mend
- Put me out of my misery
- A nervous wreck
- Nip and tuck
- A nip-and-tuck race
- Nurse a drink
- Nurse a grudge
- Opiate of the masses
- Feeling no pain
- No pain, no gain
- A pain in the neck
- Racked with pain
- Share your pain
- Painful silence
- Growing pains
- Take great pains
- A painstaking task
- A patient who is a hard stick
- A bitter pill
- Be a pill
- A poison pill
- Take a chill pill
- A tough pill to swallow
- Avoid him like the plague
- Choose your poison
- Poison the well

State of shock

- She's ready to pop
- Love potion
- A pox on both your houses
- A pregnant pause
- The best prescription for that is
- Psyched out
- Break out in a rash
- A rash decision
- Feeling run-down
- On the safe side
- It gives me the shivers
- State of shock
- Sticker shock
- A shot in the arm
- See a shrink

- Sick and tired
- Sick at heart
- Take a sick day
- Worried sick
- In sickness and in health
- It's nothing to sneeze at
- Get it out of your system
- Get the full treatment
- The silent treatment
- Tailor your treatment
- Vim and vigor
- Go viral
- A worrywart
- Warts and all
- Mean well
- Well-off
- Do a workup
- The walking wounded
- Lick your wounds
- Open old wounds
- Self-inflicted wounds
- Time heals all wounds
- Wounds run deep

MILITARY & WEAPONS

1.

2.

1. Fall on your sword   2. Hit the target

- More arrows left in the quiver
- Swift as an arrow
- Slings and arrows
- To bomb
- Bombs away
- Photobomb someone
- A ticking time bomb
- Get bombed
- Drop a bombshell
- Bite the bullet
- Dodge the bullet
- The magic bullet
- Take a bullet for him
- Cannon fodder
- A loose cannon
- Hold a club over their heads
- Caught in the crosshairs
- Caught in the crossfire
- Fire at will
- Fire away
- Friendly fire
- Hold your fire
- In the line of fire
- On the firing line
- Jump on the grenade
- Find the smoking gun
- Going great guns
- Gun down
- Gun for someone
- Hold a gun to his head

- Jump the gun
- A son of a gun
- Stare down the barrel of a gun
- Stick to your guns
- Under the gun
- Call shotgun
- A shotgun wedding
- Take the hit
- Cut like a knife
- On a knife-edge
- Get loaded
- Loaded for bear
- Loaded language
- Locked and loaded
- Lock, stock, and barrel
- Hoist by your own petard
- With pinpoint accuracy
- Keep your powder dry
- Sitting on a powder keg
- Saber rattling
- Shell-shocked
- An offshoot
- Shoot daggers
- Shoot down the legislation
- Shoot first and ask questions later
- Shoot from the hip
- Shoot to kill
- Shoot me down
- Shoot the bull

- Shoot the messenger
- Shoot the works
- Shoot your mouth off
- Shoot yourself in the foot
- A straight shooter
- Sure as shootin'
- The whole shooting match
- A big shot
- A buckshot approach
- Call the shots
- Give it a shot
- Give it your best shot
- A fair shot
- I'm shot
- Not by a long shot
- A parting shot
- A scattershot approach
- A shot across the bow
- Shot heard 'round the world
- A shot out of the blue
- Shots fired
- It's worth a shot
- Slay it
- At sword's point
- Cross swords
- A double-edged sword
- Fall on your sword
- Swords into ploughshares
- Damn the torpedoes, full speed ahead

- Finger on the trigger
- Pull the trigger
- Quick on the trigger
- Trigger an event
- Trigger-happy
- Trigger warning
- A weapon of choice
- Crack the whip
- A call to action
- A piece of the action
- See action
- A ragtag army
- You and whose army?
- Don't ask, don't tell
- Command attention
- Snap to attention
- To the barricades!
- Battle lines are drawn
- A battle of nerves
- The Battle of the Bulge
- A battle of wills
- Battle royale
- A battle to end all battles
- Fight a losing battle
- Fight your own battles
- Man your battle stations
- It's a never-ending battle
- On the battlefield
- It's only half the battle
- Pick your battles

Don't bring a knife to a gunfight

- A pitched battle
- Prepare for battle
- A running battle
- A seesaw battle
- An uphill battle
- To win the battle but lose the war
- A bunker mentality
- Captain Obvious
- Behave in a cavalier manner
- Lead the charge
- Code red
- Your wish is my command
- Divide and conquer
- Stoop to conquer
- Take cover
- It defeats the purpose

- Snatch victory from the jaws of defeat
- The last line of defense
- Attention to detail
- Duty calls
- Above and beyond the call of duty
- In the line of duty
- I wouldn't wish it on my worst enemy
- You're your own worst enemy
- Don't bring a knife to a gunfight
- Fight it out
- Fight or flight
- Fight to the bitter end
- Fight the good fight
- A fight to the finish

It takes two to fight

- It takes two to fight
- Itching for a fight
- Live to fight another day
- Pick a fight
- A rough-and-tumble fight
- Spoiling for a fight
- A fighting chance
- In fighting trim
- Them's fightin' words
- A false-flag operation
- Flag something
- Be flagging
- Keep the flag flying
- Take flak

- A force to be reckoned with
- A show of force
- Hold down the fort
- A united front
- Throw down the gauntlet
- Caught off guard
- A changing of the guard
- Don't let your guard down
- Lower your guard
- In harm's way
- Don't be a hero
- Hero worship
- An unsung hero
- Hold steady

- A badge of honor
- A code of honor
- Act with honor
- Do the honors
- On my honor
- Be at liberty
- Go on maneuvers
- Get your marching orders
- March in lockstep
- March on
- Steal a march on
- With might and main
- With military precision
- Mission creep

- On a mission
- A search-and-destroy mission
- Pass muster
- At peace
- Hold your peace
- Keep the peace
- Make peace with
- Peace out
- Smoke the peace pipe
- Rally 'round the flag
- Rally the troops
- Break ranks
- Close ranks
- Join the ranks
- Pull rank
- The rank and file
- Rise through the ranks
- At the ready
- I'm as ready as I'll ever be
- Ready for action
- A rebel without a cause
- Mount a resistance
- Salute the colors
- The opening salvo
- It served its purpose
- A lonely soldier
- A soldier of fortune
- To soldier on
- Take a stab at
- A standoff

- Strike against
- Hit the target
- A moving target
- On target
- Don't tread on me
- In the trenches
- Send in the troops
- Swear like a trooper
- Call a truce
- In the vanguard
- An act of war
- An all-out war
- Beat the drums of war

- The culture war
- Been in the wars
- An old warhorse
- On a war footing
- On the warpath
- The spoils of war
- A tug-of-war between
- A war of words
- The war to end all wars
- A war without end
- It's a war zone
- A happy warrior

Take a stab at

MONEY

The almighty dollar

- Biggest bang for your buck
- Break the buck
- The buck stops here
- Hard to make a buck
- Know how to make a buck
- Pass the buck
- Trying to save a buck
- Make the big bucks
- Burn through cash
- A cash cow
- Cash in
- Cash is king
- Cash out
- Cash poor
- Flush with cash
- Pool of cash
- Pressed for cash
- Rake in the cash
- Ready to cash it in
- Stash your cash
- Strapped for cash
- Ten cents on the dollar
- That and fifty cents will get you a coffee
- A two-cents plain
- Chump change
- Change to spare
- A nice chunk of change
- Get short-changed
- Check out

- Get a blank check
- Keep in check
- A reality check
- Checks and balances
- Earn your paycheck
- Live paycheck to paycheck
- Coin a phrase
- Play both sides of the coin
- Gain wide currency
- At the drop of a dime
- It's a dime a dozen

Play both sides of the coin

- Drop a dime
- Move off the dime
- Stop on a dime
- Turn on a dime
- The almighty dollar
- Another day, another dollar
- Sound as a dollar
- A day late and a dollar short
- A dollar and a dream
- The best that money can buy

- Blood money
- Come from old money
- Dirty money
- Do anything for money
- Easy money
- Follow the money
- A fool and his money are soon parted
- Found money
- Get your money's worth
- Given a run for your money

- In the money
- It takes money to make money
- A license to print money
- Mad money
- He's made of money
- Make money hand over fist
- Money burns a hole in my pocket
- Money doesn't grow on trees
- Money for jam

- Money for old rope
- Money going up in smoke
- It's like money in the bank
- Money is the root of all evil
- Money pit
- Money talks
- Money to burn
- The money train
- Money well-spent
- A money-spinner
- More money than sense
- My money is on you
- New money
- On the money
- Pin money
- It's like pouring money down the drain
- Put money on
- Put money on the table
- Put your money where your mouth is
- Rake in the money
- Right on the money
- Seed money
- Show me the money
- Sit on your money
- Spend money as if there's no tomorrow
- Take the money and run
- There are some things money can't buy

- Throw money at it
- Throw good money after bad
- Throw money out the window
- A ton of money
- Didn't have a nickel to my name
- Don't take any wooden nickels
- To be nickel-and-dimed
- A nickel tour
- Not worth a plug nickel
- That and a nickel will get you on the subway
- It's your nickel
- He doesn't have two nickels to rub together
- Bright as a new penny
- In for a penny, in for a pound
- It cost a pretty penny
- A penny for your thoughts
- Penny-ante
- A penny-pincher
- Turn up like a bad penny
- Useless as a penny
- Worth every penny
- It's like pennies from heaven
- Give no quarter
- Split the bill
- A bank shot
- Break the bank
- Don't bank on it
- Laugh all the way to the bank
- A run on the bank

- You can take that to the bank
- Break open the piggy bank
- Bankroll someone
- Beg, borrow, or steal
- Beggars can't be choosers
- Go broke
- Go for broke
- Make a bundle
- Cha-ching!
- Cheap laughs
- Cheap thrills
- Do it on the cheap
- It doesn't come cheap
- Sometimes cheap is too expensive
- Cheaper by the dozen
- At any cost
- The cost of living
- At all costs
- It costs a bundle
- Forever in your debt
- I owe you a debt of gratitude
- Tackle deficits
- I've got dibs!
- Get your due
- Spare no expense
- Get your fiscal house in order
- Cost a bloody fortune
- Free for the asking
- Free time

- A free-for-all
- Get a free ride
- Get a free pass
- A freeloader
- All present and accounted for
- By all accounts
- Held accountable
- A vested interest
- In the interest of time
- Invest in yourself
- Filthy lucre
- In the lap of luxury
- Make allowances for
- Charge what the market will bear
- Play the market
- The ups and downs of the market
- You haven't paid your dues
- Don't pay it any mind
- You get what you pay for
- Hit pay dirt
- It'll pay dividends
- Pay a visit
- Pay as you go
- Pay attention
- Pay back in kind
- Pay down your debt
- Pay heed
- Pay homage
- Pay hush money

- Pay it forward
- Pay off
- To pay on advance
- Pay your own way
- Pay out of pocket
- Pay the piper
- Pay the ultimate price
- Pay through the nose
- Pay to play
- Pay top dollar
- Pay under the table
- Pay your respects
- Down payment
- It pays for itself
- Make a poor showing
- Poor as a church mouse
- The poor devil
- A poor man's version
- Everyone has their price
- Have a price on your head
- It comes at a price
- The price is right
- That's the price you have to pay
- Quote a price
- There's a price to pay
- At any rate
- At this rate
- Filthy rich
- The rich get richer
- Soak the rich

- Stinking rich
- Too rich for my blood
- Nouveau riche
- An embarrassment of riches
- From rags to riches
- Get it on sale
- Scrimp and save
- Dip into your savings
- Sell the family silver
- Sold for a song
- Spend it all in one place
- It's a steal
- A stock phrase
- Pick up the tab
- Put it on my tab
- Run a tab
- A tax write-off
- Taxing situation
- By the same token
- Take its toll
- Trade up
- True value
- Let the moths out of your wallet
- Lighten one's wallet
- Share the wealth
- Spread the wealth
- More trouble than it's worth
- Not worth the trouble
- Take it for what it's worth
- Worth diddly-squat

NAMES & PEOPLE

1.

2.

3.

1. A wingman 2. He's a jack-in-the-box 3. Cry like a baby

- An honest Abe
- Nice thinkin', Abe Lincoln
- Achilles' heel
- Adam's apple
- We don't know you from Adam
- Built like an Adonis

Don't throw the baby out with the bathwater

- The adult in the room
- A smart aleck
- A Horatio Alger story
- She's all that
- She's the genuine article
- Atta boy!
- Atta girl!
- The baby boomers
- Baby needs a new pair of shoes
- Baby steps
- Cry like a baby
- A crybaby
- Don't throw the baby out with the bathwater

- Left holding the baby
- Soft as a baby's bottom
- He's a teddy bear
- The belle of the ball
- A Benedict Arnold
- Spend a Benjamin
- Heavens to Betsy!
- Bette Davis eyes
- Friends of Bill
- Just plain Bill
- Yes siree, Bob
- The boogeyman is going to get you
- Set up a boogeyman
- All work and no play makes Jack a dull boy
- A boy scout
- A boy toy
- A mama's boy
- Oh boy!
- A playboy
- Pretty boy
- Sad boy
- A tomboy
- The whipping boy
- Boys will be boys
- Good ol' boys
- A member of the old boys' club
- The old boys' network
- Big Brother is watching
- Brother from another mother

- My brother's keeper
- Oh, brother!
- Brothers in arms
- Buddy system
- Buddy-buddy
- Our little bundle of joy
- Like Caesar's wife
- A little Caesar
- Raise Cain
- A happy camper
- A Casanova
- A castaway
- Chatty Cathy
- A charley horse
- A good-time Charlie
- It's child's play
- No child left behind
- The poster child
- Spare the rod and spoil the child
- Join the club
- Welcome to the club
- A Collyer's mansion
- Wrong Way Corrigan
- A motley crew
- Beat the crowd
- Far from the madding crowd
- Play to the crowd
- Stand out from the crowd
- Custer's Last Stand

- Sword of Damocles
- Dapper Dan
- Dashing Dan
- A Daniel in the den of lions
- David and Goliath
- Davy Jones's locker
- Debbie Downer
- He's a dimwit
- A cool dude
- To each his own
- A little Einstein
- Elvis has left the building
- All in the family
- She's like family
- One of the family
- What is said in the family stays in the family

A gentlemen's gentleman

Play the fool

- Father knows best
- Like father, like son
- A Faustian bargain
- Bye, Felicia

- To be a clean-cut fellow
- A fishwives' tale
- In like Flynn
- An old fogy
- Make a fool of someone
- Nobody's fool
- On a fool's errand
- Play the fool
- Played for a fool
- Tomfoolery
- He doesn't suffer fools
- Frankenstein's monster
- A frenemy
- A Freudian slip
- Frick and Frack
- False friend

- A friend in need is a friend indeed
- In the friend zone
- An imaginary friend
- Fast friends
- With friends like that, who needs enemies?
- He's a fusspot
- The gang's all here
- A generation gap
- The greatest generation
- A gentleman of the old school
- A gentlemen's agreement
- A gentlemen's gentleman
- By George!
- Curious George
- Let George do it

- A cover girl
- The girl next door
- Girl power
- A golden girl
- It girl
- My girl Friday
- A pin-up girl
- A valley girl
- Girls' night out
- She is in her glory
- A go-getter
- Van Gogh's ear for music
- Take on a Goliath
- Cut the Gordian knot
- A grandfather clause
- Get grandfathered in
- Be my guest
- The guest of honor
- He's always gung ho
- A gloomy Gus
- A fall guy
- A stand-up guy
- A wise guy
- Nice guys finish last
- One of the good guys
- Pull an Al Haig
- Sign your John Hancock
- Give 'em hell, Harry
- Feuding like the Hatfields and the McCoys

- Be a hermit
- She's beside herself
- A Hobson's choice
- A modern-day Robin Hood
- A parade of horribles
- The hostess with the mostest
- Pull a Houdini
- According to Hoyle
- All too human
- He's a hunk

A fall guy

- He doesn't know jack
- Every Jack has his Jill
- He's a jack-in-the-box
- Jack of all trades, master of none
- Calamity Jane
- Me Tarzan, you Jane

- Jekyll & Hyde
- Jim Dandy
- Jimmy a lock
- The patience of Job
- A cup of joe
- G.I. Joe
- A good Joe
- Joe blow
- Joe lunchbucket
- Joe schmo
- Joe Six-Pack
- Not your average Joe
- Quality Joe
- A regular Joe
- Say it ain't so, Joe
- Dear John letter
- Go to the john
- An honest john
- John Bull
- John Doe
- John Q. Public
- A Johnny-come-lately
- Johnny one-note
- Johnny-on-the-spot
- Keep up with the Joneses
- Jones for something
- No way, José
- Just joshin' you
- She's a keeper
- The comeback kid

- I kid you not
- The new kid on the block
- A snot-nosed kid
- A whiz kid
- You did good, kid
- All kidding aside
- Just kidding
- No kidding around
- Kilroy was here
- Ladies first
- A classy lady
- The Iron Lady
- A lady of leisure
- The lady of the house
- Happy as Larry
- Lucky Lindy
- A lost cause
- You're a real MacGyver
- A mister Magoo
- Mamma mia!
- Are you a man or a mouse?
- Are you man enough?
- A broken man
- A family man
- A good man is hard to find
- A ladies' man
- The last man standing
- Leave no man behind
- Low man on the totem pole
- Macho man

- Man about the house
- Man alive!
- Man down!
- A man of the people
- Man plans, God laughs
- Man proposes, God disposes
- Man-to-man
- A man's man
- A marked man
- My main man
- No man can serve two masters
- Of no use to man or beast
- Renaissance man
- My old man
- Stand by your man
- Stick it to the man
- Take it like a man
- You're the man
- A wingman
- A yes man
- Mansplain
- A Hail-Mary pass
- Typhoid Mary
- The real McCoy
- A member of the club
- Separate the men from the boys
- A Mickey-Mouse operation
- The Midas touch
- For the love of Mike
- Holy Mike!

- Sure, Mike
- A Walter Mitty
- Montezuma's revenge
- Everyone and their mother
- Like mother, like daughter
- Your mother country
- Mother knows best
- It's the mother of all . . .
- Mr. Right
- Mr. Right Now
- No more Mr. Nice Guy
- Take a mulligan
- A mulligan stew
- Murphy's Law
- Mutt and Jeff
- A big name
- Clear your name
- Give something a bad name
- It's all in the name
- Make a name for yourself
- To name a few
- Name and shame
- Name names
- Name your price
- Smear someone's good name
- That's my name, don't wear it out
- It has your name written all over it
- Drop names
- Negative Nancy

- A Napoleon complex
- The natives are restless
- A ne'er-do-well
- A nervous Nellie
- A half nelson
- Nero fiddles while Rome burns
- A Florence Nightingale
- An old chap
- An old codger
- An old coot
- An old maid
- Open a Pandora's box
- A paragon of virtue
- A helicopter parent
- A stay-at-home parent
- Nosey Parker
- A patsy
- A pessimistic Patty
- The perils of Pauline
- All things to all people
- Have my people call your people
- My kind of people
- Level with the people
- People from all walks of life
- People of the book
- A people person
- Feel like a new person
- Be your own person
- Nothing personal

- Personality crisis
- Split personality
- For Pete's sake
- For the love of Pete
- Peter out
- Peter Pan Syndrome
- The Peter principle
- Rob Peter to pay Paul
- The Pinocchio test
- Positive Polly
- A Pollyanna
- Ponzi scheme
- The grand poobah
- My pride and joy
- She's a prima donna
- A pushover
- A pyrrhic victory
- A quisling
- A rabble-rouser
- Rebecca of Sunnybrook Farm
- A modern-day Paul Revere
- Before you can say Jack Robinson
- Rich as Rockefeller
- Jolly Roger
- Roger that
- Signing off, Roger
- Rosie the Riveter
- It's a Rubik's Cube
- Sally forth

- What in the Sam Hill is going on here?
- A Good Samaritan
- Great Scott!
- Beam me up, Scotty
- Scout's honor
- A Scrooge
- Seward's Folly
- A shirker
- Simon says
- Simple Simon
- Have the persistence of Sisyphus
- A slacker
- Solomon's choice
- The wisdom of Solomon
- A favorite son
- The return of the Prodigal Son
- The shoemaker's son always goes barefoot
- A son is a son until he takes a wife; a daughter is a daughter all of her life
- A Sophie's choice
- An old sourpuss
- Speedy Gonzales
- A spinster
- The goon squad
- Don't be a stranger
- Hello, stranger
- No stranger to
- Stranger danger

- Stranger in a strange land
- Lazy Susan
- Suzy Sunshine
- A doubting Thomas
- Every Tom, Dick, and Harry
- A troublemaker
- Tweedledee and Tweedledum
- An evil twin
- Bob's your uncle
- Everybody and their uncle
- Say uncle
- Uncle Sam
- It happens to the best of us
- VIP treatment
- Put on your Mae West
- It's not what you know, it's who you know
- Slick Willy
- A wisenheimer
- Old wives' tales
- You can't keep a good woman down
- Every woman for herself
- An everywoman
- Feel like a new woman
- I am woman, hear me roar
- A kept woman
- A self-made woman
- A take-charge woman
- Woman about town
- A woman of means

- A woman of the world
- Woman to woman
- A woman's right to choose
- A woman's work is never done
- Women and children first
- I'm with you
- In spite of yourself

You can't keep a good woman down

NATURE

1.

2.

1. *Sturdy as an oak*   2. *Bark up the wrong tree*

- The bloom is off the rose
- The bloom of youth
- A late bloomer
- Nip in the bud
- Beat around the bush
- Beat the bushes
- Cave in
- A man cave
- In clover
- Fresh as a daisy
- Pushing up daisies
- Delicate as a flower
- Flower power
- A wallflower
- Move at a glacial pace
- Live in a glass house
- Sharp enough to cut glass
- Grass grows beneath his feet

- The grass is always greener
- A grassroots movement
- On the right side of the grass
- Ground down
- Grounds for dismissal
- Grow by leaps and bounds
- Grow close
- A growth experience
- It will grow on you
- A fig leaf
- Leaf through
- Shake like a leaf
- Turn over a new leaf
- Gild the lily
- Lily-livered
- Go out on a limb
- Break a logjam
- A bump on a log
- Easy as falling off a log
- Log on
- Saw logs
- At loggerheads
- If the mountain won't come to Muhammad
- You can't fool Mother Nature
- A force of nature
- A freak of nature
- A good-natured person
- Harness Mother Nature
- It's just human nature

Between a rock and a hard place

- Let nature take its course
- Nature calls
- The nature of the beast
- Great oaks from little acorns grow
- Sturdy as an oak
- An olive branch
- A walk in the park
- Easy pickings
- Between a rock and a hard place
- Dumb as a bag of rocks
- Hard as a rock
- Rocks in your head
- Hit rock bottom
- Kick rocks
- On the rocks
- Ready to rock
- Rock it

Go out on a limb

- A rock star
- Rock the vote
- Rock your world
- A rock-ribbed conservative
- Solid as a rock
- Steady as a rock
- Get off to a rocky start
- A rocky road ahead
- A bedrock issue
- Down to bedrock
- Root and branch
- Every rose has its thorn
- Everything's coming up roses
- The last rose of summer
- I never promised you a rose garden
- It's no bed of roses
- Pin a rose on your nose
- Burn rubber
- The rubber match
- The rubber room
- Rubbernecking
- Where the rubber meets the road
- The sands of time
- Spruce up
- Beat away with a stick
- More than you can shake a stick at
- It beats a sharp stick in the eye
- Stick it out

- Carved in stone
- Cast in stone
- Cast the first stone
- Cold as a stone
- Drop like a stone
- Etched in stone
- Hit a stone wall
- Leave no stone unturned
- It's not written in stone
- Reach a milestone
- A rolling stone
- Set in stone
- A stepping-stone
- The Stone Age
- Stone-cold
- Stone dead
- Stone-deaf
- Stone sober
- Stone-faced
- A stone's throw away
- Get stoned
- Stonewall
- The touchstone
- Turn over all the stones
- Dumb as a stump
- On the stump
- Stump for someone
- Stumped
- A thorn in my side
- Shiver me timbers!

Up a tree

- Bark up the wrong tree
- Go climb a tree
- Miss the forest for the trees
- Shake someone's tree
- Swing from the trees
- Up a tree
- Ripen on the vine
- A shrinking violet
- Deep in the weeds
- Go into the weeds
- Weed it out
- A voice in the wilderness
- Get rid of the dead wood
- Knock on wood
- A babe in the woods
- Deep into the woods
- Find a way out of the woods
- Not out of the woods yet
- This neck of the woods

NICKNAMES & ACRONYMS

UFO: Unidentified Flying Object

- AKA: Also Known As
- ASAP: As Soon As Possible
- ATM: Automated Teller Machine
- AWOL: Absent Without Leave
- BAE: Before Anyone Else
- BCC: Blind Carbon Copy
- BNB: Bed and Breakfast
- BOLO: Be On the Lookout
- BYOB: Bring Your Own Beverage
- CC: Carbon Copy
- DJ: Disc Jockey
- DL: Down Low
- DM: Direct Message
- FAQ: Frequently Asked Questions
- FKA: Formerly Known As
- FOMO: Fear Of Missing Out
- FUBAR: Fouled Up Beyond All Recognition
- FWIW: For What It's Worth
- FYI: For Your Information
- GI: Government Issue
- GOAT: Greatest Of All Time
- GOP: Grand Old Party
- GPS: Global Positioning System
- ID: Identification
- IM: Instant Message
- IOU: I Owe You
- IQ: Intelligence Quotient
- IRA: Individual Retirement Account

- JK: Just Kidding
- KIA: Killed In Action
- KISS: Keep It Simple, Stupid
- KOW: Kindly Oblige With
- KP: Kitchen Police
- LASER: Light Amplification by Stimulated Emission of Radiation
- LMK: Let Me Know
- LOL: Laugh Out Loud
- MIA: Missing In Action
- MP: Military Police
- N/A: Not Applicable
- NAFTA: North American Free Trade Agreement

- NASA: National Aeronautics and Space Administration
- NATO: North Atlantic Treaty Organization
- NIMBY: Not In My Backyard
- NSFW: Not Safe For Work
- PAC: Political Action Committee
- PHD: Doctor of Philosophy
- PIN: Personal Identification Number
- PPS: Post-Postscript
- PS: Postscript
- PSA: Public Service Announcement
- R&D: Research and Development

PSA: Public Service Announcement

- R&R: Rest and Relaxation
- RADAR: Radio Detection And Ranging
- RINO: Republican In Name Only
- ROFL: Rolling On the Floor Laughing
- ROY G. BIV: Red, Orange, Yellow, Green, Blue, Indigo, Violet
- RSVP: Répondez S'il Vous Plaît
- SCUBA: Self-Contained Underwater Breathing Apparatus
- SNAFU: Situation Normal, All Fouled Up
- SONAR: Sound Navigation Ranging
- SOP: Standard Operating Procedure
- SOS: Save Our Ship
- SRO: Standing Room Only
- TBA: To Be Announced
- TBD: To Be Determined
- TGIF: Thank God It's Friday
- TLC: Tender Loving Care
- UFO: Unidentified Flying Object
- VIP: Very Important Person
- XOXO: Hugs and Kisses
- YOLO: You Only Live Once

SCUBA: *Self-Contained Underwater Breathing Apparatus*

NUMBERS

1.

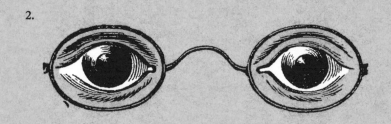

2.

3.

1. First out of the gate 2. Four eyes 3. Count on it

- All for naught
- Of no consequence
- Bar none
- Have none of it
- Amount to nothing
- It's better than nothing
- Get nothing in return
- Good for nothing
- I got nothing
- Here goes nothing
- Much ado about nothing
- Not for nothing
- Nothing but trouble
- Nothing of the kind
- Nothing special
- You are nothing if not . . .
- From zero to sixty
- Start from ground zero
- A zero-based budget
- Zero hour
- Zero in
- A zero-sum game
- Zero tolerance
- Get zilch
- The one percent
- Drawn and quartered
- The better half
- A half a loaf is better than none
- Half a mind to
- The half of it

- He's half the man
- Half-cocked
- How the other half lives
- The other half
- Take half measures
- Too clever by half
- You can't be half-pregnant
- Go halfsies
- Halfway decent
- I'll meet you halfway
- All for one and one for all
- Come one, come all
- Each one worse than the last
- Easy as 1, 2, 3
- The old one-two
- A good one
- It takes one to know one
- It's not a one-way street
- Look out for number one
- My one and only
- Number one with a bullet
- One and done
- The one and only
- One and the same
- One at a time
- One by one
- A one-day wonder
- One fell swoop
- One for the money
- One for the road

- One last drink
- One of a kind
- One step ahead
- One step at a time
- One step forward, two steps back
- One thing led to another
- One way or another
- One-way ticket
- A one-banana problem
- A one-hit wonder
- A one-horse town
- A one-liner
- A one-man show
- A one-off
- A one-shot deal
- A one-trick pony
- One-two punch
- One-up someone
- Public enemy number one
- Fool me once, shame on you; fool me twice, shame on me
- Give a once-over
- Once and for all
- Once bitten, twice shy
- At first blush
- Draw first blood
- First among equals
- First and foremost
- First-class treatment
- First come, first served

- First dibs
- A first impression
- The first lady
- First out of the box
- First out of the gate
- First things first
- First-class citizen
- First-rate
- First-timer
- Not my first rodeo
- Of the first order
- On a first-name basis
- Right of first refusal
- Take the first crack at it
- In a single blow
- Newly single
- Single out
- Single-minded
- Add your two cents
- Your number two
- A bird in the hand is worth two in the bush
- Two bits
- Feel like two cents
- Two hoots and a holler
- Go number two
- Two strikes against you
- Kill two birds with one stone
- There's no two ways about it
- Of two minds

Two can play that game

- Put two and two together
- Two can play that game
- Two for the price of one
- Two of a kind
- Like two peas in a pod
- Two schools of thought
- It's a two-way street
- A two-dimensional character
- Two-faced
- It's a two-horse race
- A two-time loser
- A two-timer
- The best of both worlds
- You and me both
- The odd couple
- A double agent
- Double as
- Double back
- A double bill
- A double bind
- Double booked
- A double-cross
- Double-deal
- Double-dip

- Double down
- Double or nothing
- A double standard
- A double take
- Double talk
- Double-time
- Double trouble
- Double up
- A double whammy
- Doubled over
- Live a double life
- Make mine a double
- On the double
- Pull double duty
- See double
- Don't give it a second thought
- Have second thoughts
- There's no second act
- Play second fiddle
- Second banana
- A second bite of the apple
- A second chance
- To second-guess
- Second in command

- A second look
- Second nature
- A second set of eyes
- Second string
- Second to none
- A second wind
- Treated as a second-class citizen
- Don't think twice
- Phony as a three-dollar bill
- Three sheets to the wind
- Three strikes and you're out
- A three-time loser
- Get the third degree
- The third rail of politics
- The third time's the charm
- The third wheel
- A third-world country
- A triple threat
- The four-one-one
- Four eyes
- Four on the floor
- A four-bagger
- A four-letter word
- On all fours
- The fourth estate
- A five o'clock shadow
- The five-finger discount
- A five-star resort
- Give me five

Behind the eight ball

- Take five
- High-fived
- A fifth column
- The fifth estate
- A fifth wheel
- Take the fifth
- Deep-six
- Six degrees of separation
- Six feet under
- Six of one, half a dozen of the other
- Six-pack abs
- Six ways to Sunday
- At sixes and sevens
- A sixth sense
- Sail the Seven Seas
- A seven-day wonder
- The seven-year itch
- In seventh heaven

- The seventh-inning stretch
- Behind the eight ball
- A cat has nine lives
- Nine days' wonder
- Nine times out of ten
- Nine to five
- On cloud nine
- The whole nine yards
- The ninth circle of hell
- Hang ten
- A perfect ten
- He's a ten
- I wouldn't touch that with a ten-foot pole
- At the eleventh hour
- Fifteen minutes of fame
- Talk nineteen to the dozen
- The nineteenth hole
- A twenty-one-gun salute

- A catch-22

- Twenty-four seven

- Forty winks

- To get eighty-sixed

- 100 percent effort

- For the hundredth time

- The eight-hundred-pound gorilla

- A thousand-yard stare

- The sixty-four-thousand-dollar question

- Look like a million bucks

- A million-dollar smile

- A million to one that it will happen

- Never thought in a million years

- One in a million

- Thanks a million

- An all-out effort

- All the more reason to

- All the same

- All things considered

- The be-all and end-all

- Have it all

- Not all there

- Cancel each other out

- Cancel someone

- Count noses

- Count on it

- Count sheep

- Down for the count

All the same

- You can count on me

- Counted out

- Stand up and be counted

- But who's counting?

- Get someone's digits

- Break even

- Go a few rounds with

- To infinity and beyond

- By all means

- A means to an end

- To the nth degree

- Do a number on you

- Have his number

- Hit the numbers

- Lowball the number

- Your number is up

- You're number one

- Take a number

- Your days are numbered

- By the numbers

- Crunch the numbers

- The numbers don't lie

- A numbers game

- Play the numbers

- Safety in numbers

- Strength in numbers

- Odd man out

- Odds and ends

- Sum and substance

- For the umpteenth time

- Add up

- Divide up

ON & OFF

- Act on
- Add on
- Based on
- Bear on
- Bent on
- Bring it on
- Call on
- Cotton on
- To drag on
- Draw on
- Dump on
- Dwell on
- Exact revenge on
- Fixate on
- Focus on
- A fresh take on
- Get a handle on
- Get a move on
- Get on it

- Get right on it
- Go easy on
- Go on and on
- Hang on
- Have something on your person
- Head on
- Hinge on
- Hit on
- Hold on
- It's on
- It's on me
- Keen on
- Keep calm and carry on
- Keep tabs on
- Latch on to
- Lean on
- Let him loose on it
- Make good on
- On a whim
- On account of
- On behalf of
- On fleek
- On grade
- On guard
- On it
- On show
- On site
- On the contrary
- On the cusp
- On the dole

Pile it on

- On the fritz
- On the loose
- On the off chance
- On the rise
- On the sly
- On with the show
- Pick up on
- Pile it on
- Press on
- Put the kibosh on
- Reflect on
- Right on
- A run on something
- Take him on
- Take pity on
- Try on
- Turned on
- Weigh on your mind
- And so on and so forth
- Waiting on you
- I'm onto you
- Hit upon

Lean on

- Impress upon
- Press upon
- Put upon
- Seize upon
- Take something upon oneself
- On again, off again
- On and off
- A bit off
- Beg off
- Bounce an idea off someone
- Bump him off
- Cast off
- Cordon off
- Fend off
- Finish off
- Go off book
- Go off without a hitch
- Goof off
- Hit it off

- Knock it off
- A knockoff
- Laugh it off
- Lay off
- Lead off
- A little off
- Make off with
- Mooch off
- Nod off
- Off course
- Off-kilter
- Off-limits
- Off-site
- Off the charts
- Off the hook
- Off the rack
- Off to a solid start
- Off with the fairies
- Polish it off
- Pop off
- Pull it off
- Quick off the mark
- Rattle off
- Ripped off
- Rub off on
- Run off
- Sell off
- Set someone off
- Shake it off
- Shrug it off

- Siphon off
- A spin-off
- Sponge off
- Take a load off
- Take off
- A takeoff on
- Taper off
- Tip off
- Toss off
- Turned off
- Walk off
- Ward off
- Way off

Nod off

POLITICS

The seat of power

- Reach across the aisle
- Work both sides of the aisle
- The ayes have it
- Score a bill
- A no-holds-barred campaign
- On the campaign trail
- A smear campaign
- A hanging chad
- A brokered convention
- Dirty politics
- Dirty tricks
- He couldn't be elected dogcatcher
- A political attack dog
- A congressional watchdog
- A political underdog
- A lame duck
- A clean sweep in the elections
- Give a ringing endorsement
- Big government
- The old guard
- Influence peddling
- Lead from behind
- Lead from the front
- Take me to your leader
- The far left
- Left of center
- He's the mayor of this town
- A needle in a haystack
- The party faithful

- The party line
- Broaden the base
- The political will
- Make political hay
- A political agenda
- Political asylum
- A political chess game

- A political circus
- Political correctness
- A political firestorm
- A political football
- Political gridlock
- A political hack
- A political hot potato

The old guard

- Political jockeying
- A political junkie
- A political machine
- A political pawn
- Score political points
- A politician on the take
- All politics is local
- Backroom politics
- Gotcha politics
- Leave your politics at the door
- Old-school politics
- Play politics
- Politics as usual
- Politics makes strange bedfellows
- Pork-barrel politics
- Put politics aside
- Have veto power
- More power to you
- A power struggle
- The powers that be
- The seat of power
- Tip the balance of power
- A Teflon president
- For the public good
- The far right
- Right of center
- Work the room
- A spoiler
- Where you stand depends on where you sit

- A blue state
- The deep-state theory
- The nanny state
- Purple state
- A red state
- A sad state of affairs
- Separation of church and state
- Count on your support
- The tyranny of the majority
- Get out the vote
- A swing vote
- Vote with your feet
- Vote your pocketbook
- You have my vote
- Voter fatigue

The nanny state

POSTAL

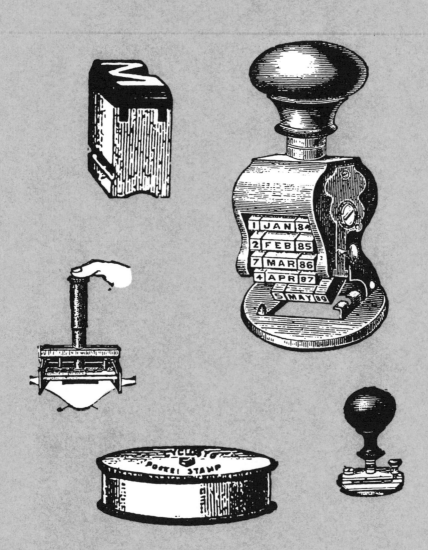

Rubber-stamp it

- Delete someone
- The envelope, please
- Push the envelope
- Take a letter
- The check is in the mail
- Junk mail
- Mail it in
- Send a message
- It's part and parcel
- A pen pal
- Posthaste
- Go postal
- Keep me posted
- Return the favor
- A seal of approval
- Seal the deal
- Sealed with a kiss
- Signed, sealed, and delivered
- Give someone a send-off
- Press "send"
- Of a sort
- All sorts of problems
- Give a stamp of approval
- Rubber-stamp it
- Stamp out

It's part and parcel

RELIGION & SPIRITUALITY

- Baptism by fire
- Beggar belief
- Cling to your beliefs
- Contrary to popular belief
- Bible-thumping
- Of biblical proportions
- Swear on a stack of bibles
- Be blessed
- A blessing and a curse
- A blessing in disguise
- Count your blessings

- A divine right
- An act of faith
- An article of faith
- Blind faith
- A breach of faith
- A crisis of faith
- In good faith
- Keep the faith
- A leap of faith
- Lose faith
- Oh ye of little faith

- For the love of God
- God bless you
- A god complex
- God help us all
- As God is my witness
- God only knows
- God willing
- God's gift to man
- The god's honest truth
- A godsend
- Godspeed
- In the lap of the gods
- Put the fear of God in you
- What in God's name
- Why on God's green earth
- Your God-given right
- Don't take it as gospel
- The gospel truth
- Fall from grace
- Grace me with your presence
- A grace period
- The saving grace
- Stay in his good graces
- There but for the grace of God go I
- Holier than thou
- The Holy City
- Holy cow!
- The Holy Grail
- Holy Moses!
- The holy of holies

Holier than thou

- A mixed blessing
- Give credence to
- A cross to bear
- Cult of personality
- Divine intervention

- Show bad faith
- A show of good faith
- An act of God
- Don't play God
- Don't tempt the gods

Preaching to the choir

- A holy terror
- Holy Toledo!
- An unholy alliance
- False hope
- Next year in Jerusalem
- It's kosher
- In limbo
- Lord it over him
- The Lord works in mysterious ways
- Meet your maker
- The whole megillah
- At the mercy of
- Throw yourself on someone's mercy
- A minor miracle
- A miracle worker
- Take the moral high ground
- Rest in peace
- Is the Pope Catholic?
- The answer to a maiden's prayer
- You're in my prayers
- He doesn't have a prayer

- Preach, sister
- Preaching to the choir
- Reach the Promised Land
- A self-fulfilling prophecy
- Use the bully pulpit
- Get religion
- The religious right
- Wear your religion on your sleeve
- A rite of passage
- A sacred cow
- A sacrificial lamb
- He's no saint
- The patience of a saint
- A patron saint
- It's a sign
- A cardinal sin
- It covers a multitude of sins
- Pay for the sins of
- A penitent sinner
- Sin City
- A sin of omission
- Ugly as sin

- Bare your soul
- Do some soul-searching
- A genuine old soul
- Good for the soul
- A good soul
- Keep body and soul together
- A lost soul
- My soul mate
- A poor soul
- Salve for the soul
- Save his soul
- Sell your soul
- A wise old soul
- If the spirit moves you
- In good spirits
- Kindred spirits
- Mean-spirited
- That's the spirit
- A wish come true
- Word from on high
- Worship at the porcelain altar
- Worship the ground you walk on

RHYMES

1. Zip it, lock it, put it in your pocket.   2. Fancy-schmancy
3. Good night, sleep tight, don't let the bedbugs bite

Boys and their toys

- Ants in your pants
- Beat a retreat
- Better skadoodle, poodle
- Boys and their toys
- By hook or by crook
- Chew your food, Gertrude
- Chillin' like a villain
- Coulda, woulda, shoulda
- Dennis the Menace
- Different strokes for different folks
- A Don Juan
- Easy peasy
- Even Steven
- Fancy-schmancy
- Finders keepers, losers weepers
- Fuddy-duddy
- Gal pal

- Geez Louise
- Girls rule, boys drool
- Gloom and doom
- Good night, sleep tight, don't let the bedbugs bite
- Hanky-panky
- Haste makes waste
- Heebie-jeebies
- Helter-skelter
- Hibby jibbies
- Hobnob
- Hocus-pocus
- Hodgepodge
- Hoi polloi
- Hoity-toity
- Hokeypokey
- Hotsy-totsy
- Huff and puff

- Hurly-burly
- Hustle and bustle
- Jeepers creepers
- Keep it in the tub, bub
- Keep it off the table, Mabel
- Kowtow
- Large as a barge
- Later, tater
- Loosey-goosey
- A man with a plan
- Mary, Mary, quite contrary
- Mumbo-jumbo
- Nitty-gritty
- No muss, no fuss
- Odd Todd
- Okey-dokey
- Okey-dokey, smokey
- Pell-mell

Gloom and doom

See you later, alligator. In a while, crocodile.

- Phoney-baloney
- A pill mill
- A plain Jane
- Razzle-dazzle
- Ready, Betty?
- Ready, Freddy?
- Rinky-dink
- Roly-poly
- See you later, alligator. In a while, crocodile.
- See you soon, you big baboon
- Shake and bake
- Sharing is caring
- Shop till you drop
- A silly Billy

- A silly Millie
- Silly-dilly
- Snitches get stitches
- Snug as a bug in a rug
- Steady Eddie
- Step on a crack, break your mother's back
- Suck it up, buttercup
- Superduper
- Take a break
- Take care, teddy bear
- That's a fact, Jack!
- The bee's knees
- The real deal
- Tricky Dick

- Use it or lose it
- Used and abused
- What's the plan, Stan?
- What's your number, cucumber?
- When in doubt, throw it out
- Why so sad, Chad?
- Willy-nilly
- Your nearest and dearest
- Zingers that linger
- Zip it, lock it, put it in your pocket

ROYALTY

A crowning touch

Topple the crown

- A robber baron
- A man's home is his castle
- Build castles in the sand
- Castles in the air
- Chamber of horrors
- To crown it all
- The crown jewels
- The crown prince
- It's a jewel in the crown
- Lose your crown
- Topple the crown
- Uneasy lies the head that wears the crown
- Crowned
- A crowning achievement
- Your crowning glory
- A crowning moment
- A crowning touch
- Duke it out
- Put up your dukes
- The emperor has no clothes

- An heir apparent
- A court jester
- Fit for a king
- In the country of the blind, the one-eyed man is king
- The king of the castle
- King of the hill
- The king of the mountain
- King of the ring
- The King of Swing
- King's money
- A king's ransom
- Live like a king
- Speak the King's English
- Treated like a king
- Who died and made you king?
- For want of a nail, the kingdom was lost
- My kingdom for a horse
- Thy kingdom come
- Pay a kingly price

- A kingmaker
- A knight in shining armor
- A lady-in-waiting
- Palace intrigue
- Pomp and circumstance
- Fit for a prince
- Prince Charming
- A princely sum
- She's a little princess
- A beauty queen
- Fit for a queen
- Queen of hearts
- A queen's ransom
- Treated like a queen
- A regal presence
- Get a royal sendoff
- Get the royal treatment
- Your royal highness
- A royal pain
- A royal screwup
- The royal "we"
- A royal welcome
- Loyalty before royalty
- Treated like royalty
- Rule the roost
- Rule with a velvet glove
- The power behind the throne
- The woman behind the throne
- Yeoman's service

SCIENCE & TECHNOLOGY

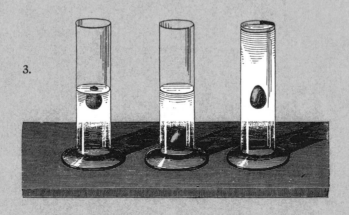

1. Under the microscope 2. In free fall 3. A test case

- The acid test
- Be basic
- Back to basics
- Your biological clock is ticking
- A buffer zone
- Carbon footprint
- A catalyst for growth
- All charged up
- Recharge your batteries
- There's no chemistry between them
- Baked into the DNA
- It's part of your DNA
- Brave the elements
- In your element
- Out of his element
- A bundle of energy
- A controlled experiment
- The human experiment
- A thought experiment
- By force of circumstance
- By force of habit
- The driving force
- In free fall
- The gene pool
- Reinvent the wheel
- Reinvent yourself
- To make matters worse
- Under the microscope
- Create a monster

- In perpetual motion
- Go nuclear
- The nuclear option
- Suck the oxygen out of the room
- Proof positive
- A quantum leap
- Blind them with science
- Have it down to a science
- It's not rocket science
- The sweet science
- A makeshift solution
- Take up space
- A waste of space
- Give off a lot of static
- Suspension of disbelief
- Pass the litmus test
- Put it to the test
- A test case
- Send up a trial balloon
- The trial-and-error method

- Channel surf
- Clickbait
- Crack the code
- A computer crash
- A computer glitch
- Cyber Monday
- Failure to launch
- Cast a wide net
- A safety net
- Fall off the radar
- On the radar
- Under the radar
- Radio silence
- Rise like a rocket
- All systems go
- Technically speaking
- Telegraph your plan
- A beta test
- On the same wavelength

Rise like a rocket

SENSES

Take a look in the mirror

- Fall on deaf ears
- Turn a deaf ear
- Can't hear myself think
- You could hear a pin drop
- Hear from someone
- Hear ill of someone
- Hear tell of
- Hear you out
- I hear you
- Now hear this
- When you hear hoofbeats, think horses, not zebras
- Heard through the grapevine
- Listen to your body
- Listen up
- The art of listening
- Loud and proud
- Peace and quiet
- Break your silence
- A conspiracy of silence
- The silence is deafening
- Silent as the grave
- Silent killers
- The silent majority
- On sound footing
- Safe and sound
- A sound bite
- Sound off
- Sound out
- Sound the alarm

- Sounds good to me
- Sounds like a plan
- A joy to behold
- Lo and behold
- The blind leading the blind
- Blind luck
- Blind spot
- Blind with love
- Go on a blind date
- Robbed you blind
- Willful blindness
- Blindsided
- Gaze into a crystal ball
- He won't meet my glance
- The spitting image of
- Don't look a gift horse in the mouth
- Don't look for trouble
- Don't look now
- If looks could kill
- Look after
- Look askance
- Look high and low
- Look me in the eyes
- Look on the bright side
- Look put-together
- Look the other way
- Look up to
- Made you look
- Make someone look good

- Never look back
- A new look
- Take a long look
- Take a look in the mirror
- She's a looker
- Looking dapper
- Looking sharp!
- Look through rose-colored glasses
- Things are looking up
- Looks can be deceiving
- Peek and shriek
- A sneak peek
- You can see it from space
- I know a good thing when I see it
- I see what you did there
- I thought I'd never see the day
- If you see something, say something
- A must-see
- Nothing to see here, folks
- Now you see it, now you don't
- We'll see about that
- See after
- See how it plays out
- To see it is to believe it
- See it through
- See over the horizon
- See stars

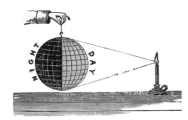

See the light of day

- See the light of day
- See through someone
- See to something
- See you when I see you
- Wait and see
- What you see is what you get
- You have to see it to believe it
- Seeing is believing
- You ain't seen nothing yet!
- Children should be seen and not heard
- You haven't seen the last of me
- That remains to be seen
- I've seen it all
- It's seen its day
- Seen with the naked eye
- You should've seen the other guy!
- Show your cards
- Hiding in plain sight
- In plain sight
- No end in sight
- No relief in sight
- Out of sight

- Out of sight, out of mind
- A sight for sore eyes
- A sight to behold
- Sight unseen
- She's a sorry sight
- Show foresight
- Hindsight is 20/20
- Hindsight is always easier
- Shortsighted
- Raise sights
- Set our sights on
- Stare into space
- Steal a glance
- Not on my watch
- Watch him like a hawk

- Watch the birdie
- Watch your mouth
- Watch your step
- It's like watching paint dry
- It doesn't pass the smell test
- Smell a rat
- Smell blood
- The smell of the lamp
- Smell out
- Smell trouble
- Smell victory
- The sweet smell of success
- Come out smelling like a rose
- Sniff out
- An acquired taste

Show your cards

- Have good taste
- In bad taste
- In poor taste
- It left a bad taste in my mouth
- It left a bitter taste in my mouth
- No accounting for taste
- A question of taste
- Taste blood
- A taste of your own medicine
- A taste test
- Close contact
- Keep in contact
- Have contacts
- Feel for someone
- Feel it in my bones
- Feel left out
- Feel small
- Feel the pinch
- Feel the squeeze
- Get a feel for
- Put out feelers
- Have mixed feelings
- Not feeling it
- Feel all the feels
- Gloss over something
- Handle something
- No hard feelings
- Grief pain
- Come through in a pinch
- It'll do in a pinch

- Help out in a pinch
- Rub the wrong way
- Scratch my back
- Scratch one's head
- Scratch out a living
- Scratch the surface
- Start from scratch
- A softie
- My main squeeze
- Put the squeeze on someone
- Have sticky fingers
- It's a sticky situation
- Tickle the mind
- Tickle your fancy
- An easy touch
- The finishing touch
- Have a common touch
- Have a perfect touch
- Have a velvet touch
- A healing touch
- Just the right touch
- Keep in touch
- A light touch
- Lose touch
- Lose your touch
- A magic touch
- It needs a female touch
- It's a nice touch
- Only touch the surface
- Out of touch

- A personal touch
- A soft touch
- Stay in touch
- Touch a chord
- Touch a raw nerve
- It's touch and go
- Touch bottom
- Touch down
- A touch of class
- Touch screen
- Touch the sky
- Touch up
- Touch upon
- A touch-tone system
- Be touched
- Everything he touches turns to gold
- Have all the right touches
- Put on the finishing touches
- It's very touching
- A touchy subject
- Touchy-feely
- Common sense
- He doesn't have a lick of sense
- Have a sense of balance
- Lack common sense
- Make sense of something
- It makes no sense
- It makes sense
- Come to your senses

SHAPES, LINES & POINTS

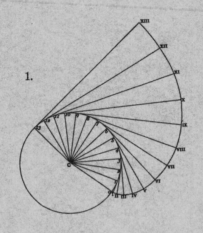

1.

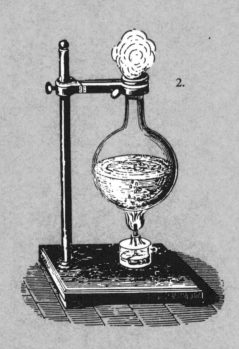

2.

- Never miss an angle
- Try a different angle
- Play all the angles
- Circle back
- The circle of trust
- Circle the wagons
- Close the circle
- Come full circle
- A member of the inner circle
- A vicious circle
- Go around in circles
- Move in the right circles
- Talk in circles
- Ahead of the curve
- Throw a curve
- On the dot
- Connect the dots
- Edge out
- Hard-edged

Go around in circles

- Have an edge
- Lose your edge
- On edge
- On the bleeding edge
- On the edge
- On the leading edge
- Over the edge
- Take the edge off
- Rough around the edges
- At loose ends
- Make ends meet
- Cut a fine figure
- Figure it out
- Go figure
- Flat broke
- Form follows function
- True to form
- The assembly line
- A bloodline
- Cross the line
- Cut the line
- A dividing line
- Drop me a line
- The end of the line
- Fall in line
- The family line
- A fine line between
- A gig line
- Hold the line
- In line for

Hold the line

- It's all on the line
- Jump the line
- Kept in line
- Lay it on the line
- A line item
- A line of thought
- A lot is on the line
- Off-line
- On the front line
- Out of line
- Over the line
- Somewhere along the line
- Take a hard line
- Throw someone a line
- Top of the line
- To toe the line
- Walk a fine line
- Walk the line
- Where to draw the line?
- Your baseline
- Lined with
- A hard-liner
- Along the same lines
- Along those lines

- Blur the lines
- Stay within the lines
- Close the loop
- Keep in the loop
- Knocked for a loop
- Loop back around
- Out of the loop
- That's beside the point
- The boiling point
- Come to the point
- From point A to point B
- Game point
- Get to the point
- Inflection point
- A low point
- Match point
- There's no point
- On point
- Past the point of no return
- Point-blank range
- The point man
- The point of diminishing returns
- A point of view
- The point person
- A pressure point
- Prove a point
- I see your point
- A selling point
- Starting point

- Stretch the point
- Take point
- The tipping point
- To the point
- A turning point

Earn your stripes

- Up to a point
- A vantage point
- What's the point?
- Sticking points
- Talking points
- Get around to something
- Jerk someone around
- Make the rounds
- Bent out of shape
- In bad shape
- In good shape
- Not in any way, shape, or form
- Out of shape
- The shape of things to come

- Shape up
- Take shape
- Whip into shape
- A slant rhyme
- On the spot
- Spot-on
- A tight spot
- Back to square one
- Come out foursquare for
- Get your three squares
- A square
- A square deal
- A square meal
- Square off
- A square peg in a round hole
- Square the circle
- All squared away
- Give it to me straight
- Keep a straight face
- Let me get this straight
- On the straight and narrow
- A straight arrow
- Straight as an arrow
- A straitjacket
- Of every stripe
- Earn your stripes
- Show your stripes
- Off on a tangent
- Vertically challenged
- Give it a whirl

SLEEP & DREAMS

Sleep like a baby

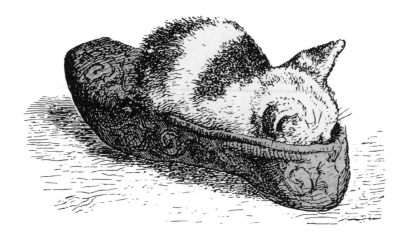

Take a catnap

- Asleep at the switch
- Asleep at the wheel
- Fast asleep
- Half-asleep
- Sound asleep
- I'm beat
- Doze off
- Chase a dream
- Daydream
- It's like a dream
- Dream big
- Dream catcher
- A dream come true
- A dream date
- Dream on
- A dream team
- A dream ticket
- Dream up
- Dream up a plan
- Dream weaver
- A dreamboat
- Dreamy
- Live in a dream world
- Livin' the dream
- A pipe dream
- I wouldn't dream of it
- Dreamers and doers
- A dreamer
- Beyond my wildest dreams
- Broken dreams
- Chasing your dreams
- Don't give up on your dreams
- Follow your dreams
- In your dreams
- Pursue your dreams
- The stuff of dreams
- Sweet dreams
- That's what dreams are made of
- Exhaust the possibilities
- I'm knackered
- Let it lie
- Lie in wait
- Take it lying down
- Caught napping
- Take a catnap
- Take a power nap
- It was a nightmare
- Your worst nightmare
- Give it a rest
- No rest for the weary
- No rest for the wicked
- Put it to rest
- Rest up
- Rest upon
- An early riser
- Sack out
- Catch up on my beauty sleep
- Cry yourself to sleep
- Didn't sleep a wink
- Don't lose any sleep over it
- Put to sleep
- Sleep away the day
- Sleep begets sleep
- Sleep in
- Sleep in his eyes
- Sleep it off
- Sleep like a baby
- Sleep like a log

- Sleep like a rock

- Sleep like a top

- Sleep on a clothesline

- Sleep on it

- Sleep out

- Sleep tight

- Sleepaway camp

- A sleepy little town

- A late sleeper

- A sleeper

- A sleeper cell

- Don't poke the sleeping bear

- Let sleeping dogs lie

- Sleeping on the job

- Sleep with the fishes

- A sleepover

- A snooze-fest

- Take a snooze

- You snooze, you lose

- All tuckered out

- Awaken a sleeping giant

- A rude awakening

- Wake up and smell the coffee

- Wake up on the wrong side of the bed

- To wake up to

- It's a wake-up call

- Be woke

- Catching some Zs

Sleeping on the job

SPORTS & GAMES

1. Hit it out of the ballpark 2. Not know what hit you 3. Get a kick out of it 4. Empty the bench

- Bait and switch
- Didn't take the bait
- Fish or cut bait
- An airball
- A ball hog
- The ball is in your court
- Ball out
- A slimeball
- Carry the ball
- Drop the ball
- Follow the bouncing ball
- Get on the ball
- Get the ball rolling
- Have a ball
- Move the ball forward
- He's no ball of fire
- On the ball
- Push the ball down the field
- Run with the ball
- That's the way the ball bounces
- Throw a curveball
- Throw the ball
- A whole other ball of wax
- That's the ballgame
- A whole new ballgame
- A ballpark figure
- In the ballpark
- Spike the football
- Touch football
- He couldn't get to first base

- Cover your bases
- Off-base
- Touch base with
- Inside baseball
- Bat around an idea
- Go to bat for
- Right off the bat
- Batting a thousand
- Come from behind
- A benchmark
- A benchwarmer
- Empty the bench
- Have a deep bench
- The best offense is a good defense
- Get the best of someone
- A personal best
- Bob and weave
- Give someone a boost
- Bowled over
- Boxed into a corner
- Catch a break
- A fast break
- A tiebreaker
- Buzzer beater
- A good call
- Make a call
- The biggest catch of the day
- Be a catch
- Catch a falling star

Go to bat for

- Catch air
- Catch my ears
- Catch on
- Catch someone at a bad time
- Catch the wave
- Catch up to him
- Catch up with someone
- Catch you later
- Catch you on the flip side
- Catch as catch can
- A catchall
- A good catch
- Good catch!
- If you catch my drift
- Caught off-base
- Move the chains

A social climber

- Cut to the chase
- Checkmate
- Cheers and jeers
- A chess master
- Choke up
- Chuck it all
- A steep climb
- A social climber
- Make a comeback
- A competitive edge
- Courtside seats
- A full-court press
- Home-court advantage
- It's not cricket
- A dash of salt
- A mad dash
- A dive
- A dive bar

- Dive in
- Take a dive
- Dodge the issue
- The domino effect
- A slam dunk
- Have a field day with
- Home-field advantage
- Leave it all on the field
- Level the playing field
- Out of left field
- Come out fighting
- The finish line is in sight
- Fish for compliments
- Fish in troubled waters
- Like shooting fish in a barrel
- Go on a fishing expedition
- Flip out
- Flip through

- Flip your wig
- Get him to flip
- Cry foul
- Foul play
- No harm, no foul
- Ahead of the game
- Anyone's game
- At the top of your game
- Back in the game
- Beat you at your own game
- Bring your A-game
- Early in the game
- Fair game
- A fool's game
- I'm game
- The game is up
- A game of chance
- A game of chicken
- A game of give and take
- A game of two halves
- Game on
- Game over
- The game plan
- A game stopper
- Game the system
- A game-changer
- Game, set, match
- Get your head in the game
- He's got game
- A high-stakes game

- Late in the game
- The name of the game
- Not all fun and games
- Off your game
- On your game
- The only game in town
- A pawn in their game
- A perfect game
- A pickup game
- Play a game of hide-and-seek
- Put the game on ice
- Raise your game
- A real game of chess
- Run away with the game
- Step up your game
- Talk a great game
- The rules of the game
- What's the endgame?
- Use the glass
- A goal-line stand
- Move the goalposts
- Push it over the goal line
- A golf clap

A real game of chess

- Grandstand
- Put someone in a headlock
- Hit a grand slam
- Hit a home run
- Hit a nerve
- Hit for the cycle
- Hit it in the sweet spot
- Hit it out of the ballpark
- Hit someone up
- Hit someone where it hurts
- Hit the mark
- Hit the spot
- Not know what hit you
- Pinch hit
- A heavy hitter
- A switch-hitter
- Hold your own
- A hole-in-one
- Hook, line, and sinker
- Huddle up
- Hunt and peck
- The old hunting grounds
- On a witch hunt
- It's the last inning
- A shock jock
- Jockey for position
- To get a jump on
- Jump at the chance
- Jump for joy
- Jump into the deep end

- Jump right into it
- Jump through hoops
- Jump to conclusions
- A jumping-off point
- Jumping up and down
- The top of the key

Just for kicks

- Get a kick out of it
- Kick back and relax
- Kick in
- Kick off
- Kick oneself
- Kick-start the economy
- Kick the habit
- Kicked around
- Kicked on
- Kicked to the curb
- Kicked upstairs
- Here's the kicker
- Kicking butt and taking names
- For kicks and giggles
- Just for kicks

- Take kickbacks
- Knock yourself out
- Get knocked down and get right up
- Knocked out
- She's a knockout
- Knock it out of the park
- A layup
- Take the lead
- In a league of your own
- Major league
- Out of your league
- A bush leaguer
- In the big leagues
- Leap for joy
- Leap in the dark
- A leap year
- Take a leap
- Have something to lose
- Lose it
- A loser's limp
- A sore loser
- Nothing but net
- Out of bounds
- A change of pace
- Pace yourself
- Pick up the pace
- Put someone through their paces
- Above par
- Below par

- On par
- Par for the course
- Under par
- Up to par
- Make a pass at
- Pass over
- Pass the baton
- Take a hard pass
- This too shall pass
- Have a passing acquaintance with
- On pitch
- On the pitch
- Pitch in
- Step up to the plate
- Come back into play
- A double play
- Fair play
- Get played
- Make a play for him
- Play along
- Play ball
- Play both sides against the middle
- Play by the rules
- Play catch-up
- Play Cupid
- Play dirty pool
- Play dumb
- Play fast and loose
- Play favorites

- Play for keeps
- Play for the other team
- Play for time
- To play hardball
- Play head games
- To play hooky
- Play into their hands
- Play it close to the chest
- Play it safe
- Play it to the hilt
- Play nice in the sandbox
- Play nose tackle
- Play phone tag
- Play possum
- Play the blame game
- Play the field
- Play the game
- Play the hand you've been dealt
- Play the long game
- Play up to him
- Play whack-a-mole
- Play with heart
- Play with someone's heart
- Play your heart out
- The play-by-play
- A squeeze play
- Downplay
- Played a blinder
- Played for a sucker
- Played off

- Played out
- Well played
- The playoffs
- See how it plays out
- A pop fly
- Pop out
- Able to take a punch
- Beat him to the punch
- A counterpunch
- A knockout punch
- Land the first punch
- Pack a punch
- Punch above your weight
- Punch in
- A punch to the gut
- Punch-drunk
- Slow to the punch
- A sucker punch
- Pull no punches
- Roll with the punches
- Trade punches

Smooth sledding

- A punching bag
- Push comes to shove
- Off to the races
- A race against time
- Race through something
- A race to the bottom
- A race to the finish
- The race to the top
- It's a racket
- On the rebound
- On the receiving end
- Reel it in
- Get into the ring
- A ringside seat
- A rookie move
- A go-ahead run
- It's run its course
- Run rampant
- A walk-off home run
- A runner-up
- Tie goes to the runner
- The meter's running
- Scoot over
- Even the score
- Know the score
- Run up the score
- Score points
- Settle a score
- All set
- Set it right

- Shoot an eagle
- Shoot hoops
- A cheap shot
- A chip shot
- A shot from downtown
- Left on the sidelines
- A leadoff single
- Skate on thin ice
- Skate too close to the edge
- Don't get over your skis
- Slaphappy
- Smooth sledding
- Tough sledding
- Let it slide
- A slugfest
- A southpaw
- A sparring partner
- A bad sport
- A good sport
- An old sport
- A poor sport
- The sport of kings
- A spoilsport
- A false start
- A jump start
- Hope something sticks
- Stick it
- Down the stretch
- Strike a balance
- Strike one's fancy

- Strike out
- Strike upon
- Surf the net
- Surf the web
- A surfer dude
- Sink or swim
- Swim against the current
- Swim against the tide

Tee off

- Swim upstream
- A swing and a miss
- Swing for the fences
- Go down swinging
- Tackle a problem
- The A-team
- A crack team
- On the JV team
- Tag team

- Take one for the team
- Tee off
- Teed off
- Throw an eye on something
- Throw him a bone
- Throw up your hands
- It's a throwback
- Thrown into the deep end
- A toss-up
- Tryouts
- A major upset
- Make weight
- A sticky wicket
- You can't win 'em all
- In it to win it
- A no-win situation
- Win by a hair's breadth
- Win by a landslide
- Win by a mile
- Win by a nose
- Win by a whisker
- Win fair and square
- Win hand over fist
- Win hands-down
- Win her heart
- Win it handily
- A win-win situation
- Come out a winner
- Wrestle him to the ground
- Wrestle it from him

- Wrestle with a pig
- Wrestle with an idea
- In the zone
- In your comfort zone
- Zone out

STONES & METALS

1.

2.

1. A silver fox 2. Strike gold

Forge ahead

- Bold as brass
- Let's get down to brass tacks
- The top brass
- Make something crystal clear
- A diamond in the rough
- In fine fettle
- Forge ahead
- A gem of an idea
- A hidden gem
- A little gem of a book
- A real gem
- A crock of gold
- Fool's gold

- Go for the gold
- The Gold Coast
- A gold digger
- A gold rush
- The gold standard
- A gold star
- Good as gold
- Liquid gold
- The pot of gold at the end of the rainbow
- Sitting on a gold mine
- Solid gold
- Strike gold

- He's a goldbricker
- You're golden
- A golden age
- The golden boy
- Golden handcuffs

A hidden gem

- A golden opportunity
- A golden parachute
- The Golden Rule
- A golden ticket
- The golden years
- Have golden hands
- Silence is golden
- An iron curtain
- An iron grip
- An iron will
- An iron-clad agreement
- Rule with an iron fist
- Strong as iron
- Irons in the fire
- Jaded
- Heavy as lead
- It went over like a lead balloon
- Heavy metal
- Metal mouth
- A metalhead
- Show some mettle
- Undermine authority
- Like quicksilver
- A bit rusty
- Above the salt
- Back to the salt mines
- An old salt
- A pinch of salt
- Rub salt into the wound
- Salt away

- The salt of the earth
- Take it with a grain of salt
- Worth its salt
- A salty old dog
- A salty tongue
- Handed everything on a silver platter
- A silver bullet
- A silver fox
- The silver screen
- Hard as steel
- A steel magnolia
- Steel yourself
- True as steel
- Steely-eyed

Handed everything on a silver platter

STREETS, ROADS & PATHS

1.

2.

1. In a jam   2. At a crossroads

- Go down a blind alley
- Right up your alley
- Explore all avenues
- He's been around the block more than once
- A blockbuster
- Off the blocks
- Bridge the gap
- A bridge to nowhere
- A bridge too far
- You'll cross that bridge when you come to it
- Build bridges
- Hit a speed bump
- Lose your moral compass
- Backed into a corner
- Corner the market
- A cornerstone
- Go to your corner
- In his corner
- Put in a corner
- Right around the corner
- Turn the corner
- Highway robbery
- A highway to hell
- Highways and byways
- My way or the highway
- The information superhighway
- In a jam
- All over the map
- Back on the map

- Given a road map
- Lay down a road map
- Put it on the map
- Cross paths
- Go down the wrong path
- Off the beaten path
- A path forward
- The path of least resistance
- A proven path
- Pave the way
- Pound the pavement
- No easy off-ramps
- Ramp up
- At a crossroads
- A bump in the road

- Don't go down that road
- The end of the road
- For the road
- I've been down that road before
- Hit the road
- Hit the road, Jack
- Look down the road
- Make inroads
- On the road
- A road hog
- Road rage
- A road to nowhere
- The road to recovery
- A road warrior
- The rules of the road

On the road

Throw them off the trail

- Treat and street
- Happy trails
- Throw them off the trail
- Trail off
- A trailblazer
- Take a turn for the better
- Take a turn for the worse
- By the way
- Find your way
- Get your way
- Go your separate ways
- In the way
- Lead the way
- Lose your way
- Make way
- Make your own way
- Part ways
- A roundabout way
- Set in one's ways
- That's the way it is
- Fall by the wayside
- Underway

- Stick to the road
- Take the high road
- Take the low road
- Take the middle road
- Take the road less traveled
- A tough road ahead
- A turn in the road

- Depends which side of the street you're on
- On easy street
- Street-smart
- The streets are paved with gold
- Streetwise
- Take to the streets

TIME & AGE

Take time out to smell the roses

- Give me a second
- Not a second too soon
- Occur in a split second
- Secondhand information
- At the last minute
- In a minute
- Just a minute
- A laugh a minute
- Minute by minute
- An aha moment
- Caught up in the moment
- The defining moment
- A senior moment
- Just a moment, please
- A magical moment
- May I have a moment of your time?
- The moment of truth
- Never a dull moment
- Not a moment too soon
- On the spur of the moment
- Seize the moment
- At a moment's notice
- A momentary lapse in judgment
- Your finest hour
- Happy hour
- Hour of need
- The man of the hour
- Off-hours
- Rush hour

- The witching hour
- After hours
- For hours on end
- There aren't enough hours in the day
- Up until all hours
- The wee hours of the morning

He doesn't know the time of day

- At the end of the day
- Back in the day
- Let's call it a day
- Carry the day
- Clear as day
- D-day
- The day got away from us
- Day in, day out
- The day is young
- A day of reckoning
- He doesn't know the time of day
- From day one
- The good old days
- A banner day

- Honest as the day is long
- In my day
- In this day and age
- You made my day
- Make a day of it
- Make my day
- Not your day
- One day at a time
- It's plain as day
- Rue the day
- Save the day
- Take forever and a day
- Take it day by day
- Tomorrow is another day
- He wouldn't give me the time of day
- Be in your heyday
- The days of wine and roses are over
- It's early days yet
- Glory days
- He's seen better days
- Those were the days
- Here today, gone tomorrow
- Today is not your day
- A daily basis
- A needle in a haystack
- Up-to-date
- A morning person
- Morning, sunshine
- Call it a night

- The night is young
- Obvious as night turning to day
- Things that go bump in the night
- That's what keeps me up at night
- Pull an all-nighter
- It didn't happen overnight
- An overnight success
- In our Sunday best
- Sunday blues
- Sunday driver
- Sunday funday
- Throw a Sunday punch
- It won't happen in a month of Sundays
- A Monday-morning quarterback
- Throwback Thursday
- Friday the thirteenth
- Beware the Ides of March
- Mad as a March hare
- March madness
- April showers bring May flowers
- A May-December romance
- Mayday! Mayday! Mayday!
- For everything there is a season
- It's open season
- The four seasons
- A man for all seasons
- In the dead of winter
- Old Man Winter

- Winter blues
- Hope springs eternal
- Spring ahead, fall back
- Spring back
- Spring fling
- Spring for it
- Spring something on somebody
- Spring to mind
- Spring up like mushrooms
- A springboard
- It's time for spring cleaning
- An Indian summer
- A summer fling
- Summer slide

Buy time

- The waning days of summer
- Fall all over yourself
- Fall apart
- Fall into place
- Fall into disuse
- Fall prey to
- Fall to pieces
- Take the fall for
- A fallback plan

- Advanced in years
- Down through the years
- Getting up in years
- Turn of the century
- History in the making
- History repeats itself
- The rest is history
- There's always a first time
- Behind the times
- It's about time
- Ahead of time
- Ahead of your time
- All in due time
- All in good time
- Beat back Father Time
- Before your time
- Bide your time
- Buy time
- Call a time-out
- Caught in a time warp
- Crunch time
- Do hard time
- Doing time
- Don't do the crime if you can't do the time
- For quite some time
- For the time being
- From time immemorial
- From time to time
- Frozen in time

- In real time
- In record time
- In the fullness of time
- In the nick of time
- In the right place at the right time
- In the wrong place at the wrong time
- In time
- In times like these
- It takes time
- Keep track of time
- Kill time
- Lag time
- A legend in his own time
- Live on borrowed time
- It's been a long time coming
- Long time no see
- Long time no talk
- Lose track of time
- Make good time
- Make time
- Make time with someone
- Make up for lost time
- Make up time
- Mark time
- There's no time like the present
- There's no time to lose
- Not ready for prime time
- It's as old as time
- On one's own time

In time

- Full time
- Give someone a hard time
- Go back in time
- A grand old time
- A bang-up time
- A time of it

- All the time in the world
- Downtime
- Have the time
- Have time on your hands
- In next to no time
- In no time at all

Time's up

- On time
- Once upon a time
- It's only a matter of time
- Only time will tell
- Pass the time
- It's payback time
- Perfect timing
- Play out over time
- A point in time
- Pressed for time
- Quality time
- Right on time
- Run out of time
- Save time
- Spare time
- Stood the test of time
- Stuck in time
- Take time out to smell the roses
- Take your own sweet time
- Take your time
- There's a time and place for everything

- A time capsule
- A time crunch
- Time flies
- Time flies when you're having fun
- Time in a bottle
- Time is money
- The time is now
- Time is of the essence
- Time is on your side
- Time is precious
- The time is ripe
- Time is running out
- Time limit
- Time marches on
- Time off for good behavior
- A time sink
- A time suck
- Time to kill
- Time to move on
- Time to take off the gloves
- Time works wonders
- Time-consuming
- A time-honored tradition
- A time-share
- Told time and time again
- Turnaround time
- A waste of time
- While away the time
- You can't turn back time

- It's your time
- Your time has come
- Time's a wastin'
- Time's up
- An old timer
- Change with the times
- Desperate times call for desperate measures
- Fall on hard times
- Get with the times
- In tune with the times
- Keep up with the times
- Let the good times roll
- Many times over
- May you live in interesting times
- A sign of the times
- The spirit of the times
- These are demanding times
- It's tough times
- For old times' sake
- Bad timing
- Timing is everything
- Age before beauty
- Age is just a number
- Age out
- That awkward age
- Come of age
- Feel your age
- Middle age
- New age

- The tender age
- Underage
- It's been ages
- That's one for the ages
- Of old
- You're only as old as you feel
- An old bag
- Old enough to know better
- The old switcheroo
- The old-fashioned way
- Ripe old age
- Same old, same old
- An oldie but a goodie
- Youth is wasted on the young
- Young and foolish
- Young at heart
- Youngblood
- A young chick
- A young Turk
- A young whippersnapper
- Drop behind
- Fall behind
- Get behind something
- Put something behind you
- In for the duration
- A has-been
- Late out of the gate
- Late to the party
- What have you done for me lately?

- It's later than you think
- Better late than never
- It's never too late
- Will wonders never cease?
- You've never had it so good
- A blast from the past
- A checkered past
- Don't dwell on the past
- Live in the past
- Mired in the past
- The past is prologue
- Past its prime
- A thing of the past
- A voice from the past
- At your earliest convenience
- Early to bed, early to rise
- It's still early
- In a jiffy
- Brand spanking new
- Good as new
- The new normal
- New to the game
- It's old news
- What else is new?
- Every now and again
- From now on
- Now and then
- It's now or never
- Who's crying now?
- None too soon

- It's too soon to tell
- Sooner rather than later
- Keep after
- Take after
- Every so often
- Give someone pause
- It's not if but when
- When you least expect it

TOOLS, HARDWARE & GEAR

1.

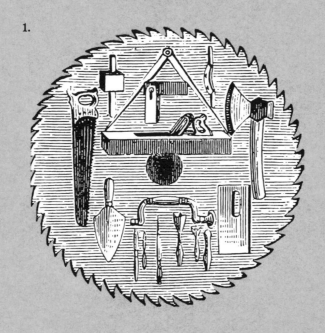

2.

A hatchet job

- An ax to grind
- A battle ax
- Get the ax
- Waiting for the ax to fall
- Chisel away
- Chisel someone out of something
- Clamp down
- Put a damper on it
- Drill down
- A drill sergeant
- Know the drill
- File it away
- Drop the hammer
- Go at it hammer and tongs
- Go under the hammer
- Hammer away
- Hammer it down
- Hammer it home

- Hammer it out
- Hammer on
- Use a big hammer on a small nail
- Get hammered
- Take a hammering
- A hammerlock
- Dumber than a bag of hammers
- Hit them with a sledgehammer
- Take a sledgehammer to it
- Fly off the handle
- Get a handle on it
- Bury the hatchet
- A hatchet face
- A hatchet job
- Get on my level
- On the level
- Ratchet it up
- An old saw
- Scrape by
- Scrape together
- Pick-and-shovel work
- Shovel-ready
- When the shovel hits the dirt
- Not the sharpest tool in the shed
- Tool around
- Tool up
- Another tool for your toolbox
- The tools of the trade
- A gut-wrenching story

- Heart-wrenching
- A wrenching experience
- In a bind
- The ties that bind
- Bit by bit
- Every bit helps
- Bolt
- Sit bolt upright
- The nuts and bolts
- Hook me up
- Let off the hook
- Off the hook
- Get hooked on
- Get your hooks in
- On tenterhooks
- The linchpin
- Hit the nail on the head
- The final nail in the coffin
- Nail him to the wall
- Nail it
- Nail it down
- Nail the suspect
- Hard as nails
- Mad enough to spit nails
- Tough as nails
- Taken down a peg
- Has him pegged
- Pull the plug
- Keep plugging away
- A screw loose

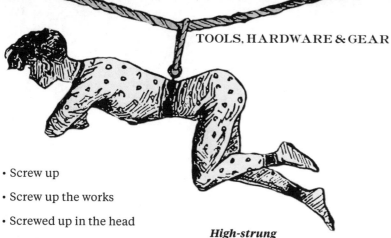

High-strung

- Screw up
- Screw up the works
- Screwed up in the head
- Put the screws on
- Tighten the screws
- Sharp as a tack
- Try a different tack
- Bulldoze someone
- Break the chain
- The chain of command
- Chain-smoking
- Off the chain
- The old ball and chain
- Yank someone's chain
- Claw your way back
- Claw your way to the top
- Crank it out
- Left to your own devices
- Stick like glue
- Come unglued
- Glued to someone
- At the bottom of the ladder
- Climb the corporate ladder
- Climb the ladder of success
- Only as strong as its weakest link
- A cog in the machine

- The hype machine
- A well-oiled machine
- All hands to the pump
- Prime the pump
- Carry a rope in your pocket
- At the end of your rope
- Give him enough rope to hang himself
- A rope-a-dope strategy
- Walk a tightrope
- Roped in
- Roped into it
- Know the ropes
- On the ropes
- Show the ropes
- A shellacking
- Pick up the slack
- Slack off
- String along
- A string of losses
- A string of victories
- String up
- No strings attached

- Pull strings
- High-strung
- A tinderbox
- All wax and no wick
- Wind it up
- Wound tight
- Down to the wire
- A loose wire
- Haywire
- A high-wire act
- Under the wire
- Hardwired
- Get your wires crossed
- Pull some wires
- Set off the trip wires
- To make a dent in something
- You can't hack it
- Hack it
- Tinker with
- Whittle away

TOP & BOTTOM

On the bottom rung

- At the top of my lungs
- Can you top this?
- Can't top that
- Off the top of my head
- On top
- Over the top
- Stay on top of it
- Tip-top shape
- Top-down
- Top-flight
- Top gun
- Top-heavy
- Top it off
- Top-notch
- Top o' the morning
- The top of the heap
- The top of the hour
- The top of the inning
- Top of the line
- The top of the pecking order
- Top off
- Top quality
- Top rate
- Top secret
- Top tier
- Top up
- Top-shelf
- From top to bottom
- A bottom feeder
- The bottom is falling out

- The bottom line
- The bottom of the hour
- The bottom of the inning
- Bottom out
- Bottoms up!
- From the bottom of my heart

- Get to the bottom of it
- On the bottom rung
- Start at the bottom

Top-shelf

TOYS

1.

2.

3.

1. Seesaw 2. Be someone's puppet 3. She's my baby doll

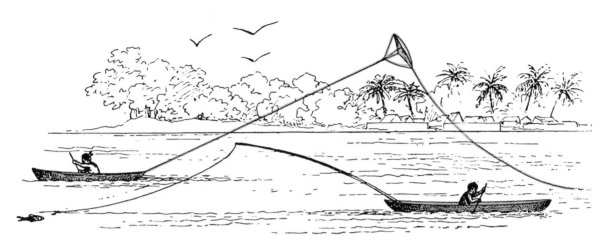

Go fly a kite

- A chip off the old block
- Boomerang child
- She's my baby doll
- She's a doll
- She looks like a Barbie doll
- All dolled up
- Go fly a kite
- High as a kite
- Have all your marbles
- Marbles in your mouth
- Lose your marbles
- Play for all the marbles
- Monopoly money
- Be a piñata
- Be someone's puppet
- Seesaw
- Like a kid with a new toy
- Toy with someone's feelings
- Toy with the idea
- Toyed with
- Throw your toys out of the pram
- Toys in the attic
- Yo-yo

TRANSPORTATION & TRAVEL

Fall off the wagon

- A flight of fancy
- In full flight
- Take flight
- Fly by the seat of your pants
- It won't fly
- A frequent flyer
- A high-flyer
- Flying blind
- Flying solo
- To be a copilot
- On autopilot
- Rail against
- Get run out of town on a rail
- Go off the rails
- Railroad something through
- Railroad someone
- Bum a ride
- A bumpy ride
- Enjoy the ride
- Get a full ride
- Hang on for the ride
- Have an easy ride
- Hitch a ride
- In for a rough ride
- Let it ride
- Ride a tiger
- Ride herd over
- Ride it out
- Ride the waves
- A ticket to ride

- Ride for the brand
- Riding high
- Be there every step of the way
- In lockstep
- Out of step
- Put a spring in your step
- A step above the rest

Flying solo

- A step ahead
- Step aside
- Step back
- A step behind
- Step-by-step
- Step down
- Step in

- Step in it
- A step in the right direction
- Step into the breach
- Step it up
- Step on it
- Step on toes
- Step out
- Step right up
- Step up
- Go take a hike
- Take steps
- A good track record
- The inside track
- Lose track of
- On the fast track
- On the right track
- On the same track
- A one-track mind
- Stay on track
- Track him down
- Get sidetracked
- Cover your tracks
- From the wrong side of the tracks
- Make tracks
- Stopped in his tracks
- Right train, wrong track
- The gravy train
- Heading for a train wreck
- Lose your train of thought

- The train is already in motion
- The train is leaving the station
- Go underground
- Subway series
- Travel light
- The well-traveled road
- A fellow traveler
- Safe travels
- Bad news travels fast
- Fall off the wagon
- Hitch your wagon to a star
- Jump on the bandwagon
- Not an easy wagon to pull
- Off the wagon
- On the wagon
- The paddy wagon
- Pull the wagon
- Pull your own wagon
- He doesn't walk on water
- Take a long walk off a short pier
- Walk all over
- Walk and chew gum at the same time
- Walk before you can crawl
- Walk in step
- Walk it off
- The walk of shame
- Walk on broken glass
- Walk the talk
- Walk with a halting gait

- You can't just talk the talk, you have to walk the walk
- Get your walking papers
- Not all who wander are lost
- A wandering eye
- A cog in the wheel
- Set the wheels in motion
- Training wheels
- Break away
- Far and away
- Get away from it all
- Get carried away
- A million miles away
- A runaway train
- Up, up, and away
- Nice getaway sticks
- Cross the great divide
- Cross the Rubicon
- The crossroads of the world
- Avenue of escape

- The details escape me
- Escape notice
- It escapes me
- Fast-forward
- In the fast lane
- Not so fast
- Faster than the eye can see
- Get back on track
- Get there
- Off the grid
- Let your conscience be your guide
- A busman's holiday
- On holiday
- A roman holiday
- In vacation mode
- Overstay your welcome

The train is already in motion

A maiden voyage

- A staycation
- A maiden voyage
- Leave it alone
- Leave it behind
- Leave no tracks
- Ready to roll
- Roll back
- Roll in the aisles
- Guilt trip
- A drug trip
- A trip down memory lane
- In a bad way
- Make your way
- We're well on our way
- Carry excess baggage
- Carry on
- A carry-on

- Fetch and carry
- Chug along
- Get off track
- Gridlocked
- Pack light
- Time to pack it in
- Send him packing
- Packs a wallop
- To move in slow motion
- Slow your roll
- Slowpoke
- Stumble upon
- I can't take it anymore
- You can't take it with you
- I can't take you anywhere
- Take a walk down the primrose path
- Take it or leave it
- Stop-and-go traffic
- Tie up traffic
- Traffic in something
- What the traffic will bear

Carry excess baggage

UP & DOWN

1. Bring it up to snuff 2. Stick up for 3. Go down easy

- All riled up
- Back it up
- Back someone up
- Back up
- Break up
- Brighten up
- Bring it up to snuff
- Buddy up to
- Bumped up
- Call up to the majors
- You can't make it up
- Caught up
- Caught up in the minutiae
- Chat up
- Clear up
- Close up
- Come up with
- Conjure up
- Cozy up to
- Crack up
- Dap someone up
- Divvy up
- Draw up
- Dummy up
- Ease up
- Empty up there
- Empty up top
- Fill up
- Flare up
- Get your hopes up

- I've had it up to here
- Hang up your spurs
- Hard up
- Hatch up
- Held up
- Hold up over time
- How are you holding up?
- Hurry up and wait
- Jacked up
- Juice up
- Knocked up
- Let up
- Line up
- Load up
- Lock up
- Loosen up
- Make up
- Man up
- Manage up
- Movin' on up
- Not all it's cracked up to be
- Don't let up
- On the up-and-up
- Open up
- Own up
- Pass up
- Patch up
- Perk up
- Pick up the pieces
- Pick up where we left off

- Play up
- Pucker up
- Pull up stakes
- Pumped up
- Put someone up
- Put up a front
- Put up or shut up
- Put up with it
- Rack up
- Right side up
- Right up there with
- Rile up
- Round up
- Settle up
- A setup
- Shake up
- Shook up
- Shore up
- Show up
- Sign up
- Snarl up
- Split up
- Stack up
- A startup
- Stick up for
- A suck-up
- Take it up
- Take someone up on something
- Take up with
- Tangled up in something

- Things are picking up
- Tripped up
- Trumped up
- Turn up
- Up and about
- Up and around
- Up and at 'em
- Up for grabs
- Up for something
- Up to it
- Up to no good
- Up to scratch
- Up to something
- Up to the challenge
- Up to the task
- It's up to you
- Up to your old shenanigans
- The upshot
- An upstart
- Upward mobility
- Wash up
- Wind up
- Wise up
- Working up to
- Wound up
- Wrap it up
- Slow on the uptake
- An upward trajectory
- Up and down
- The ups and downs

- What goes up must come down
- It's all downhill from here
- Bog down
- Boil down to
- Break down
- Bring down
- Cascade down
- Close down
- Crack down

Down and out

- Cut down
- Down and out
- Down but not out
- Down home
- Down in the dumps
- Down pat
- Down under
- I'm down with that
- Download
- Dumb down
- Flag down
- Get down
- Go down easy

- Hold it down
- Hunker down
- Hunt down
- Jot down
- Keep it down
- Keep something down
- Let down
- Narrow down
- On the down low
- Pat down
- Play down his fears
- Put down
- Put me down for
- Rub down
- Settle down
- A showdown
- Slow down
- Take him down
- Tamp down
- To tear down
- Throw it down
- Turn down
- Turndown service
- Weigh down
- Whittle down
- Wind down
- Give someone the lowdown

WEATHER

1.

2.

3.

1. Save it for a rainy day   2. Know which way the wind is blowing   3. Snowed under

Blown away

- Blow a gasket
- A blow-by-blow account
- Blow him away
- Blow hot and cold
- Blow it
- Blow my top
- Blow off
- Blow off steam
- Blow one's fuse
- Blow one's cork
- Blow smoke
- Blow the bank
- Blow the lid off
- Blow the whistle on
- Blow up in your face
- Blow your chances
- Blow your cover
- Blow your stack
- Blown to bits
- Blown out of the water

- Blown to kingdom come
- Blown to smithereens
- A blowout
- A blowout sale
- Come to blows
- Dealt a mortal blow
- A glancing blow
- Soften the blow
- That blows my mind
- Blown away
- Blown off the map
- Blown out of proportion
- Until it all blows over
- It's a breeze
- Shoot the breeze
- Easy breezy
- A black cloud
- A dark cloud
- Don't let it cloud your judgment
- Every cloud has a silver lining

- Like floating on a cloud
- A cloud hanging over you
- Under a cloud
- Under a cloud of suspicion
- Clouding the issue
- Clouds on the horizon
- Head in the clouds
- Walking on clouds
- A dry run
- A dry spell
- Flake on something
- Able to fog a mirror
- The fog has been lifted
- The fog of war
- In a fog
- I don't have the foggiest idea
- Foggy Bottom
- Hail from
- Hail to the Chief
- Lightning fast
- Lightning in a bottle
- Lightning never strikes the same place twice
- A lightning rod
- Greased lightning
- Ride the lightning
- The mists of time
- A needle in a haystack
- Come rain or come shine
- Don't rain on my parade

- Make it rain
- No rain, no rainbow
- A rainmaker
- A rainout
- Take a rain check
- Chasing rainbows
- It's raining buckets
- It's raining sideways
- When it rains, it pours
- Rainy day fund
- Save it for a rainy day
- Catch some rays
- A slush fund
- Pure as the driven snow
- Snow bunny
- A snow job
- Snowed under
- Thundersnow
- Snowball effect
- Any port in a storm
- The calm before the storm
- Dancing up a storm
- Kick up a storm
- The lull before the storm
- A perfect storm
- Ride out the storm
- A storm in a teacup
- A storm is brewing
- Storm out
- Take it by storm

Ride out the storm

- Take the town by storm
- Talk up a storm
- Weather the storm
- Work up a storm
- The sun will come out tomorrow
- On the sunny side of the street
- Let the sunshine in
- Like a ray of sunshine
- You are my sunshine
- Walking on sunshine
- A tempest in a teapot
- Steal someone's thunder
- Thunder across
- An all-weather friend
- A break in the weather
- A fair-weather friend
- Keep a weather eye open
- Lovely weather for ducks
- Under the weather
- Bend with the wind
- Catch wind of

- Get the wind behind your back
- Get wind of
- Go whatever way the wind blows
- Gone with the wind
- Hanging in the wind
- Knock the wind out of you
- Know which way the wind is blowing
- May the wind always be at your back and the sun in your face
- Put the wind up someone
- Something's in the wind
- Spit into the wind
- Throw caution to the wind
- Break wind
- Twisting in the wind
- Wind in your face
- A windfall
- Tilting at windmills
- Scattered to the four winds
- Winds of change are blowing
- The Windy City

WISE WORDS & ADAGES

An apple a day keeps the doctor away

- Above reproach
- All good things must come to an end
- An apple a day keeps the doctor away
- Be above the fray
- Be careful what you wish for
- Buck the trend
- Check your privilege
- Do your damnedest
- Don't get mad, get even
- Don't go there
- Don't lose your temper
- Don't take any guff
- Don't take "no" for an answer
- The ends justify the means
- Familiarity breeds contempt
- Go along to get along
- Hang tough
- He who hesitates is lost
- It is what it is
- It's a jungle out there
- Leave well enough alone
- The perfect is the enemy of the good
- Rise to the occasion
- Stick with it
- Sunlight is the best disinfectant
- Them's the breaks
- Wait for it

- What you don't know won't hurt you
- What's done is done
- Where there's a will there's a way

Buck the trend

YIN & YANG (OPPOSITES)

At opposite poles

Peaks and troughs

- All or nothing

- At opposite poles

- Back and forth

- It's the beginning of the end

- He doesn't know his right from his left

- From A to Z

- From dusk till dawn

- Give or take

- Hit or miss

- If you can't beat 'em, join 'em

- It's like night and day

- A make-or-break situation

- More or less

- Neither here nor there

- Neither in nor out

- An old head on young shoulders

- On the outside looking in

- Peaks and troughs

- Perfect to a fault

- Same difference

- Thanks, but no thanks

- This way and that

- Through thick and thin

- To and fro

- Right a wrong

- Win some, lose some

BONUS: OUR FAVORITE FAMILY EXPRESSIONS & NANA-ISMS

Look before you leap

- Actions speak louder than words
- All gussied up
- All that glitters is not gold
- All the livelong day
- It's always something
- Ass-backwards
- Better safe than sorry
- Build a better mousetrap
- Can't afford not to
- You can't fight city hall
- You can't get blood from a stone
- You can't judge a book by its cover
- You can't teach an old dog new tricks
- Can't have your cake and at it too
- He's the cat's meow
- You catch more flies with honey than with vinegar
- Caught between the devil and the deep blue sea
- Cautiously optimistic
- A child is a child
- Clean as a whistle
- Cleanliness is next to godliness
- Clear as a bell
- A cock-and-bull story
- Come hell or high water
- The company he keeps
- It cost an arm and a leg

- I could read him like a book
- Dead as a doornail
- He's a dead duck
- Do it on the q.t.
- Do unto others as you would have others do unto you
- It doesn't amount to a hill of beans
- He doesn't have a leg to stand on
- You don't know your ass from your elbow
- Don't bite off more than you can chew
- Don't bite the hand that feeds you
- Don't burn your bridges behind you
- Don't count your chickens before they hatch
- Don't cry over spilled milk
- Don't cut off your nose to spite your face
- Don't get on your high horse
- Don't judge a man until you've walked in his shoes
- Don't let any grass grow under your feet
- Don't put all your eggs in one basket
- Don't put off to tomorrow what you can do today
- Don't rest on your laurels
- Don't take it for granted

His eyes are bigger than his stomach

- Drop by
- It's a drop in the bucket
- Dumb as an ox
- He's a dumb cluck
- The early bird catches the worm
- Eat to your heart's content
- Eat up a storm
- Err on the side of caution
- Expect the unexpected
- His eyes are bigger than his stomach
- Fend for yourself
- Find your niche
- Fit as a fiddle
- I'll fix his wagon
- Forewarned is forearmed
- Free as a bird
- Get a load of that
- To give away the store
- Give him a kick in the behind
- Give it all you've got
- Give it your all

- Get a dose of your own medicine
- Get a song and a dance
- Get the bum's rush
- Go with the tried and true
- God only knows what goes on in the restaurant kitchen
- Good riddance
- He got his comeuppance
- She's a greenhorn
- Have the courage of your convictions
- I haven't seen hide nor hair of him
- I haven't seen him in a dog's age
- Heart power is stronger than horsepower
- She's highfalutin
- Hold your horses
- Honesty is the best policy
- It's a hop, skip, and a jump
- It's hot as hell
- That's a hot one
- If at first you don't succeed, try, try again
- If it's worth doing, it's worth doing well
- If you've seen one, you've seen them all
- Keeping company
- Know on which side your bread is buttered
- Life is not all peaches and cream

- Light as a feather
- Like it or lump it
- Like there's no tomorrow
- Little pitchers have big ears
- Look before you leap
- Look like the wreck of the Hesperus
- He's like a lump of clay
- You made your bed, now lie in it
- Make a mountain out of a molehill
- Make all the difference
- Make sure you have a plan B
- Man does not live by bread alone
- A method to his madness
- Mind your p's and q's
- His name is mud
- I need that like a hole in the head
- Never close the door behind you
- Never cut corners
- You're never too old to learn
- She's no spring chicken
- Not for all the tea in China
- It's not whether you win or lose, it's how you play the game
- Nothing ventured, nothing gained
- It's as old as the hills
- An old geezer
- On your last legs

- Once in a blue moon
- One bad apple spoils the whole barrel
- One hand washes the other
- Opportunity only knocks once
- An ounce of prevention is worth a pound of cure
- A penny saved is a penny earned
- Penny-wise and pound-foolish
- Practice makes perfect
- Practice what you preach
- Put a bug in his head
- Quitters never win. Winners never quit.
- You reap what you sow
- Right as rain
- The right stuff
- Right up his alley
- Like a headless chicken
- Seek and ye shall find
- Set a good example
- Shape up or ship out
- You should live so long
- Show some respect
- Skinny as a rooster
- Slow and steady wins the race
- He's slow as molasses
- He spends money like a drunken sailor
- Spill the beans
- The squeaky wheel gets the grease

There are two sides to every story

- When the going gets tough, the tough get going
- White as a sheet
- The whole kit and kaboodle
- The whole shebang
- Worth your weight in gold
- You are what you eat
- You can lead a horse to water, but you can't make him drink

- He'll stand on his head before I'll do that
- He's a stick in the mud
- It stinks to high heaven
- Straight from the horse's mouth
- Strike while the iron is hot
- Strong as a horse
- Sweet as sugar
- Take it easy
- It takes the cake
- It takes two to tango
- It's taking you a year and a day
- There are two sides to every story
- Tighter than a skinflint

- To err is human, to forgive is divine
- Too many cooks spoil the broth
- He took a shine to her
- Two heads are better than one
- Two wrongs don't make a right
- He wants the moon, the sun, and the stars
- We do what we have to do, not what we want to do
- Wet your whistle
- What do you want, egg in your beer?
- When hell freezes over
- When in Rome, do as the Romans do

Can you guess the expression each picture represents?

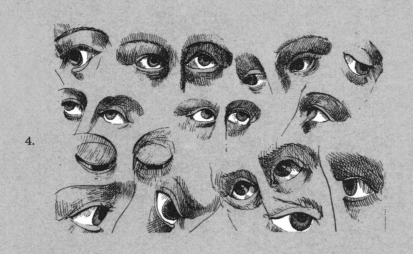

1. Poke your nose into something   2. Blow off steam   3. Wear many hats   4. All eyes on something

5. *Milk it for all it's worth* 6. *Come out of your shell* 7. *Say cheese* 8. *A sitting duck*

1. Horse around 2. Bored out of my mind 3. Proud as a peacock 4. A sad sack

5.   6.   7.   8.

5. Sticker shock   6. Piggyback on   7. Learn the ropes   8. Have time on your hands

ACKNOWLEDGMENTS

The expression **it takes a village** applies to a range of scenarios, but we'd be hard-pressed to find a situation it fits better than this book. We spent more than a decade creating this collection, and—since we didn't refer to other books as we compiled our list—our research lab consisted of the world around us. That world included passive activities like reading the *New York Times* and the *Wall Street Journal*, listening to news radio as well as public radio, and—of course—watching television and going to the movies. But we had the most fun when we were collaborating on **a daily basis** with our friends, peers, family, and all the wonderful people with whom we interacted. It was particularly gratifying when those friends would get their own spouses, partners, children, and extended family members hooked, too.

We would like to send our deepest and most sincere thanks to Colleen, Dave, Diane, Eleanor, Gideon, Janine, Jeff, Joe, Josh, Julie, Luisa, Mary, Melissa, Michele, Mike, Nelson, Preston, and Tom. We are also grateful to Dale, Deb, Janet, Jessica, Johann, John, Jonathan, Melanie, Molly, Neesha, and Zoe. Special thanks go to Danielle; to Kathy and Michael; and to Eli, Helene, and Howard. And last but not least, thanks of course to Perry, Kenneth, Miriam, Benjamin, Sarah, and Joshua—and to David, Beth, Rebecca, Adam, and Jacob.

A very special thank-you to our editor extraordinaire, Julie.

We would also like to offer our gratitude to Jon Karp, who heard our pitch more than a decade ago and offered us encouragement to **soldier on**—and to the rest of our Simon & Schuster family, who have made our **dream come true:** Theresa DiMasi, Anja Schmidt, Patrick Sullivan, Dominick Montalto, and Michael Andersen.

ABOUT THE AUTHORS

Shirley and Harold Kobliner spent more than half a century nurturing and teaching children in various settings. *So to Speak* is a reflection of their passion for education, and their deeply held belief that the best and most lasting learning is accomplished when people are having fun.

Harold received his PhD from New York University's School of Education and became a principal at the award-winning Marie Curie Junior High School, JHS 158, in Queens, New York. He was also chairman of the Board of Examiners, the independent New York City agency that created and administered tests to teachers, principals, and superintendents throughout the city. Harold's honors in the field of education span from 1955—when he was named the US Army's Soldier of the Month for creating a program for soldiers to obtain high school diplomas—to 2014, when he received City College of New York's distinguished Townsend Harris Medal for outstanding work in underserved communities.

Shirley received a bachelor of science degree in Chemistry from Queens College and was a chemistry teacher in a number of New York City high schools. She was a fierce advocate for students with disabilities, and was one of the earliest supporters of and participants in the Association for Neurologically Impaired Brain Injured Children.

Harold and Shirley raised three kids who have given them six wonderful, expressions-obsessed grandchildren. They all add up to one big family that views thinking about expressions not only as a joyful and educational exercise but also as a bonding experience.

EXPRESS YOURSELF

Here are those blank pages we mentioned at the beginning of this book. Use them to jot down expressions that we missed (and if you do, please make sure to email them to us at haroldandshirley@sotospeakbook.com). And if you have some favorite family expressions—or you want to make a few up—write them here as well. (Here's one we just invented: There's no wrong way to use a blank page.) Mostly, just have fun!

II. EXPRESSIONS: GRANDMA & GRANDPA'S
ADVICE TO THEIR GRANDCHILDREN

1. Do unto others as you would have others do unto you.
2. You can't tell a book by its cover
3. Nothing ventured, nothing gained
4. Where there's a will, there's a way
5. Seek and ye shall find.
6. A rolling stone gathers no moss
7. It's better to try and fail than not to try at all.
8. Look before you leap
9. Don't count your chickens before they're hatched
10. If at first you don't succeed, try, try again
11. The squeaky wheel gets the grease
   11A. You catch more flies with honey than with vinegar.
12. Quitters never win. Winners never quit
13. Mean what you say and say what you mean
14. You must learn to walk before you learn to run.
15. All that glitters is not gold
16. A penny saved is a penny earned
17. When you test the depth of the water, never test it with both feet
18. Never bite the hand that feeds you
19. When in Rome do as the Romans do
20. See no evil. Hear no evil. Speak no evil.

29. Fools rush in where angels fear to tread
30. By failing to prepare, you are preparing to fail.
31. People who live in glass houses shouldn't throw stones
32. The apple doesn't fall far from the tree.
33. An ounce of prevention is worth a pound of cure
34. Don't let any grass grow under your feet
35. Ambition lubricates the mind
   35A. Practice makes perfect.
36. Man does not live by bread alone
37. Don't burn your bridges behind you
38. Judge each day not the harvest you reap but by the seeds you plant.
39. God helps those who help themsel ves
40. Don't sweat the small stuff
41. When the going gets tough, the tough gets going
42. It's better to be safe than sorry
43. If you want a job done give it to a busy person
44. Don't rest on your laurels.
   44A. Don't suffer fools gladly
45. A stitch in time saves nine
46. heart power is stronger than horse power.
47. eat to live, not live to eat
48. Life is not all peaches and cream
49. Actions speak louder than words